A Consumer's Guide to
Laboratory Tests

Mary C. Ricotta, PhD

Forewords by
Adelmo P. Dunghe, MD
and
Desiree Carlson, MD

Prometheus Books
59 John Glenn Drive
Amherst, New York 14228-2197

Published 2005 by Prometheus Books

Inquiries should be addressed to
Prometheus Books
59 John Glenn Drive
Amherst, New York 14228–2197
VOICE: 716–691–0133, ext. 207
FAX: 716–564–2711
WWW.PROMETHEUSBOOKS.COM

09 08 07 06 05   5 4 3 2 1

Library of Congress Cataloging-in-Publication Data

Ricotta, Mary C.
    A consumer's guide to laboratory tests / Mary C. Ricotta.
        p. cm.
    Includes bibliographical references and index.
    ISBN 1–59102–247–9 (pbk.: alk. paper)
    1. Diagnosis, Laboratory—Popular works. I. Title.

RB37.R4975 2005
616.07'5—dc22

2004022725

Printed in the United States of America on acid-free paper.

To all clinical laboratory scientists and medical researchers who work tirelessly, often at the risk of their own health, to keep us healthy.

Contents

FOREWORD BY ADELMO P. DUNGHE, MD   11

FOREWORD BY DESIREE CARLSON, MD   13

PREFACE   15

ACKNOWLEDGMENTS   17

INTRODUCTION   19
     Why Is It Important to Know This Information?   19
     Where Are the Samples From?   20
     Who Are the Detectives behind
         Clinical Laboratory Doors?   20
     What Do You Need to Know about
         Specimens Used for Testing?   21
     Understanding the Measurements   21
     Do You Want to Know More?   22

CHAPTER 1. HOW TESTS ARE BORN   25
     Introduction   25
     Tests Are Developed   26

CONTENTS

Different Classifications for Tests 29

Coverage of Clinical Tests 31

CHAPTER 2. HEMATOLOGY 35

1. The Blood System 35
2. Cell Types 37
3. Some Tests Performed in a Hematology Laboratory 49
4. Diseases of the Blood System 55

CHAPTER 3. COAGULATION—BLOOD CLOTTING 73

1. The Coagulation System 73
2. Tests Used for Detecting Coagulation Disorders 77
3. Disorders of the Coagulation System 82

CHAPTER 4. CLINICAL CHEMISTRY 87

1. Introduction 87
2. Blood Glucose 90
3. The Renal System—Our Vital Kidneys 97
4. Calcium and Phosphorus 103
5. The Liver and Gallbladder 107
6. Purines and Uric Acid 112
7. Enzymes 114
8. Lipids—The Fear of the '90s 124
9. Proteins 131
10. The Thyroid Gland 137
11. Electrolytes 142

CHAPTER 5. MICROBIOLOGY 147

1. Introduction 147
2. Body Systems and Infections 157
3. Mycology—The Study of Fungi 172
4. Parasites That Cause Disease 176

5. Protozoa—One-Celled Parasites 179
6. Parasites That Are Flatworms and Roundworms 182
7. Viruses and Diseases They Cause 186

CHAPTER 6. IMMUNOLOGY AND SEROLOGY 199
1. A Few Facts about the Immune System 199
2. Serological Testing Principles and Some Methods 204
3. Putting the Diseases and Tests Together 209

CHAPTER 7. THE DONOR COLLECTION CENTER
      AND BLOOD BANK LABORATORY 223
1. Introduction 223
2. The Preliminaries 223
3. Blood Grouping 224
4. How Blood Groups Are Inherited 227
5. The Rh Antigen 228
6. Compatibility Testing 230
7. The Autologous Transfusion 231
8. Donor Information and Blood Components 232

CHAPTER 8. URINALYSIS 237
1. Introduction—A Common But Important Test 237
2. The Renal System 238
3. The Doctor Evaluates Test Results 239
4. Collecting the Specimen 239
5. The Test Procedures and Their Meaning 241
6. Findings in a Microscopic Examination 248

CHAPTER 9. HISTOTECHNOLOGY 253
1. The Pathology Department 253
2. Histochemical Staining of Tissues 254

CONTENTS

CHAPTER 10. CYTOTECHNOLOGY 257
1. The Papanicolaou Method 257
2. The Test Begins 258
3. The Test 260
4. The Cytotechnologist's Report 260

CHAPTER 11. MOLECULAR BIOTECHNOLOGY 263
1. Ways of Observing Our Heredity 263
2. What Is DNA? 265
3. Heredity 267
4. Characteristics of DNA Useful in Testing 269
5. Analytic Approaches to DNA Testing 270
6. Genetic Engineering—What Is It? 271
7. Gene Therapy—How Close Are We? 273

GLOSSARY 275

APPENDIX A: BODY SYSTEMS 281

APPENDIX B: CLINICAL TESTS 282

APPENDIX C: DISORDERS AND DISEASES 286

INDEX 289

Foreword

By Adelmo P. Dunghe, MD, AAFP, STFM
Attending (Emeritus),
Department of Family Medicine
State University of New York at Buffalo

In the late 1940s and early 1950s, the medical doctor made his or her diagnoses primarily with the help of clinical expertise. The laboratory support consisted of a blood sugar analysis, one blood test for kidney function, a complete blood count, and urinalysis. These would be followed by culture studies, which the medical technologists would read twice a week. By the time an autopsy was performed on a patient, we often found arteries filled with cholesterol plaque, never knowing how it got there or where it came from. Likewise, the presence of carbon in the lungs had not yet been tied decisively to smoking.

During the next ten to twenty years, however, the medical laboratory explosion began with the advent of electrolyte testing, profile panels, and the like, with no aspect of the human body ultimately escaping investigation and scrutiny. To manage this volume of knowledge, the era of specialization evolved and with it the necessity of subspecialists to handle the abundance of new procedures. Thus, the medical technician of earlier times became the clinical laboratory scientist of today.

With the information boom of the 1980s and 1990s, the patients themselves became knowledgable about their health care and its procedures, making it necessary for the medical and health communities to explain their lab results in laymen's terms.

In 1998 Dr. Mary Ricotta began writing a basic, concise text that both the patient and the health community might use to explain laboratory results and disease-related conditions. In plain English, she has organized the basic disease categories with simple discussions of the disease entities that one might expect to encounter, along with common clinical procedures and the associated laboratory studies necessary for most diagnoses.

Descriptions of body systems, laboratory procedures, organisms, cell structures, proper specimen collection and handling, and so forth are presented for easy understanding, instruction, and explanation. Although assembled primarily to provide help and understanding for the patient, this book contains a wealth of useful information that will assist the physician, the paramedic, or any other health-care provider.

As a physician, I profusely congratulate Dr. Ricotta for a job well done!

Foreword

By Desiree Carlson, MD
Chief of Pathology, Brockton Hospital
Brockton, Massachusetts

Mary Ricotta has written a much-needed book that allows the everyday consumer of health care a window into the world of laboratory medicine. From the patient's point of view, laboratory testing is like a black box. A blood or body fluid specimen is collected, testing occurs, and the physician receives some numbers. When the results are shared with the patient, he or she doesn't understand what they mean or how the physician will use them to diagnose the disease and plan treatment options.

Dr. Ricotta has broken laboratory testing down into sections of the clinical laboratory. She carefully explains how the tests are performed and what the results mean. Health-care consumers who purchase this book become empowered. They can use it to look up specific laboratory tests as needed or can sit down and read this book straight through, gaining a new appreciation of what occurs in the laboratory.

This book takes much of the mystery out of laboratory

testing. It is clear and concise. It shouldn't take the place of discussions between the patient and physician, but it can help patients formulate better questions. Patients want to be better informed. They want to feel more in control of their health care. This book will assist them in reaching these goals.

Dr. Ricotta is uniquely qualified to write this book. She has over fifty years of experience in the laboratory field as a certified medical technologist, as an active member of her professional societies, and as an educator in clinical laboratory sciences.

Preface

Each chapter in this book represents an area that is a part of clinical laboratory science. The clinical areas have within them several specialist disciplines in which a clinical scientist can practice.

As a result, there are too many tests to describe in the scope of this book. I will mention some tests that are routine for each laboratory and explain the purpose for requesting them. Because clinical tests are used to measure amounts of biochemicals that are cell products, some of my discussion is at the level of cell dynamics. However, I have written in a way that is easy to understand. If you are interested, you can delve into the mysteries of cell function when you read my references.

I have discussed briefly some of the testing techniques to inform those of you who have a scientific inclination for how we arrive at the numbers on your clinical laboratory report. Another motive of mine is a remnant of my program directorship at Daemen College in Amherst, New York—the recruitment of students to become scientists and researchers in the medical and health professions. I hope that those who are not interested in the testing details will tolerate this inclination of mine and scan those areas.

The chapters are divided into sections that should help guide you when searching for answers. When you are wondering about a particular test and you know which system is being tested, this will lead you to the clinical laboratory that performs it, and you can refer to that chapter. For example, if the test involves blood cells, you refer to the hematology chapter; if the test results indicate that the liver or kidney is malfunctioning, the reference is clinical chemistry; and if an infection is present, microbiology is consulted. In each chapter, the tests and disorders are in alphabetical order. If the test explanation is confusing, the section describing the body system can be reviewed, which may clarify things. If you know the disorder when you use the book, the last section of the chapter can be consulted.

The appendixes provide an alphabetical listing of the systems, tests, and disorders.

Acknowledgments

I would like to thank several people for their assistance in the writing of this book.

To the specialists in the various areas of laboratory medicine, both professors and practitioners, I offer my heartfelt thanks. They are Robert L. Klick, Associate Professor, Department of Biotechnical and Clinical Laboratory Sciences, State University of New York at Buffalo; Diane M. Dryja, MT (ASCP), CLS (NCA), Microbiology System Supervisor, Kaleida Health; JoAnne S. Blake, BS, MT (ASCP); and Stephen T. Koury, PhD, Director of Graduate Studies, Department of Biotechnical and Clinical Laboratory Sciences, State University of New York at Buffalo.

I especially want to thank Adelmo P. Dunghe, MD, who offered encouragement and the benefit of his long and rich experience in family practice medicine, for his review of the entire manuscript and his contributions. A pathologist and friend, Desiree Carlson, MD, deserves my gratitude for her

ACKNOWLEDGMENTS

interest and encouragement at the very early stages of the manuscript development. She also reviewed the entire work. To Gladys M. Gobbetti, who is not a scientist and who laboriously read the early manuscript when it was significantly more scientific. I am grateful for her comments.

Finally, I want to recognize Steven L. Mitchell and the people at Prometheus Books who assisted at every step of the way this first-time published author. They made it an inspiring experience.

Introduction

WHY IS IT IMPORTANT TO KNOW THIS INFORMATION?

When a physician tells you that a clinical test is needed, the first question you might think of is "Why do I need this test?" The answer is this: The physical examination and your family medical history do not provide the reason for the symptoms you experience. The information learned from a clinical test not only helps to find a diagnosis but also establishes your overall health at the same time. When the disorder is known, the type of treatment is determined by a physician. The effectiveness of treatment is guided by clinical testing, too. It is clear that clinical tests are an essential part of the science of medicine. Without testing, guesswork would prevail.

INTRODUCTION

WHERE ARE THE SAMPLES FROM?

Although we can observe physical evidence of our body metabolism, we cannot see some important things. For example, various body fluids and different types of blood or tissue cells are tested to observe their physical appearance and to measure their biochemical composition. The fluids a clinical laboratory scientist examines are usually serum or plasma, which are obtained from blood. Urine is tested in a urinalysis clinical laboratory. In the microbiology laboratory, we take specimens from the actual area that is infected. You will be surprised to know how much information these substances tell us about what is wrong. Some other substances used for testing are cerebrospinal fluid, chest fluid, joint fluid, sputum, bone marrow, feces, and hair.

A clinical laboratory scientist who specializes in examining fluids from all over the body for tumor cells is a cytotechnologist, who examines a Pap smear to find out whether cancer cells are present or developing. The Pap test that most women have done each year enables the cytotechnologist to determine whether the cells in the uterine cervix are normal. For other body sites, a smear or monolayer preparation is made of cells from those areas.

WHO ARE THE DETECTIVES BEHIND CLINICAL LABORATORY DOORS?

A variety of people take part in testing, all of whom studied subjects in the biological and chemical sciences. Many four-year-university-based programs culminate in a Bachelor of Science degree for clinical laboratory scientists. Some two-year community college programs result in an associate degree for clinical laboratory technicians. Phlebotomists are an important part of the clinical laboratory team because they obtain blood specimens from you. They may be the only one of the clinical laboratory personnel you see. The director of a clinical laboratory may be a physician pathologist or a clinical laboratory scientist with a master's or doctoral degree.

WHAT DO YOU NEED TO KNOW ABOUT SPECIMENS USED FOR TESTING?

Your physician usually depends upon clinical laboratory personnel to provide instructions for the tests requested because directions differ for each test. You may be told to fast for a certain period of time before fluid is collected. You may be given certain foods or drinks before a laboratory test, after which samples are taken. You may be required to increase or decrease fluids for a certain time before a test. If you are in doubt about what to do before a specimen is collected, call the clinical laboratory to find out the exact procedure. The accuracy of a test result depends upon the quality and quantity of the specimen to be tested.

UNDERSTANDING THE MEASUREMENTS

There is a long-standing rule among scientists that the metric system of measurement is used in all types of laboratory work and scientific research. I have assembled some of the measurements used in a clinical laboratory every day, which you will find as you read this book. They are on your clinical laboratory test report, too.

INTRODUCTION

- A millionth of a meter is a micrometer (micron—μm.), or 10^{-6} meters, or in decimals 0.000001 meters.
- A millionth of a liter is a microliter (μl.), or 10^{-6} liters, or in decimals, 0.000001 liters.
- A thousandth of a liter is a milliliter (ml.), or 10^{-3} liters, or in decimals, 0.001 liters.
- A tenth of a liter is a deciliter (dl.), or 10^{-1} liters, or in decimals, 0.1 liters.
- A thousandth of a gram is a milligram (mg.), or 10^{-3} grams, or in decimals, 0.001 grams.
- A trillionth of a gram is a picogram (pg.), or 10^{-12} grams, or in decimals, 0.000000000001 grams.

DO YOU WANT TO KNOW MORE?

Although you do not see the clinical laboratory scientist or technician performing these testing procedures, you will realize in reading this book that their tasks are critical. Their work involves the discovery of illnesses, finding out whether a treatment is effective, and making sure that the figures on a clinical laboratory report are reliable. This book takes you many steps further into the world of testing and provides you with a knowledge of numerous diseases. You will have a clear picture of what clinical testing is about and what the test values on your laboratory report mean. There is no doubt that this knowledge will help you stay healthier.

The first chapter is about how tests are developed, their regulation, and their classification. A chapter on hematology, the study of blood, follows this. There are many disorders that involve the circulating blood and bone marrow. We are all familiar with anemias, decreases in the number of red blood cells, which are a symptom of an underlying problem investigated by hematology testing. After reading this chapter, you should become familiar with the style of the book. The clinical chemistry chapter has an introduction that explains a slightly different format. The microbiology chapter is divided into a discussion of various types of microbes. Then, some information about the immune system is provided, followed by blood bank or transfusion testing. The final chapters include urinalysis, which is one of the most informative tests for physicians. The next two chapters are a brief discussion of histotechnology and cytotechnology, two vital clinical disciplines. The last chapter introduces the new and rapidly expanding testing area of molecular biotechnology.

It is my hope that in reading this book and referring to it regularly, you will understand medical terms better and become informed about clinical laboratory tests so that you understand their meaning. At the same time, my hope is that your appreciation of these dedicated professionals will increase. They perform their tests day and night in medical laboratories all over the world to improve our health.

chapter 1

How Tests Are Born

INTRODUCTION

I t is important to know not only why clinical tests are performed and what the results mean but also how they come
about. Usually a need is recognized by the medical community for the detection of a certain disease or condition. For
example, tests were needed to pinpoint molecular markers for
cancer or diabetes. A new area of testing was developed,
namely, molecular biotechnology, which allows us to find the
gene responsible for these disorders.

Some of the common clinical laboratory tests that you are
familiar with measure substances in the blood such as sugar,
urea, carbon dioxide, proteins, and so on. All these substances
that clinical scientists quantitate in laboratories are called *analytes*. It should be noted that the federal government classifies
some clinical laboratory tests with medical devices, such as

pacemakers and little instruments for measuring analytes in the comfort of your home. All of this will be discussed shortly.

TESTS ARE DEVELOPED

Some of the current tests performed in clinical laboratories are complex, and, for their development, they require the cooperation of companies that make diagnostic substances and research laboratories in academic institutions. In this type of cooperative effort, the molecular marker for breast cancer was found.

Another type of test that was developed in this way is a method for finding diabetes. It allows us to detect the disorder by testing for the glucose (sugar) values in a particular part of hemoglobin, which is in red blood cells. In contrast, the time-honored traditional way to test for sugar is by finding the amount of it in the bloodstream. The newer testing method gives us more information about how sugar is treated by a person's metabolism.

Some of the steps that take place during the joint effort of diagnostic companies and university research laboratories include the need for a test is realized; then, an idea for the test procedure is conceived by a scientist working in the laboratory; the test is developed; clinical trials are conducted; US Food and Drug Administration (FDA) approval is sought; and finally, the new test or medical device is marketed. This procedure can take several years.

Home Testing Can Be Informative

Different manufacturers of medical devices actively work on new tests for patients to monitor their health at home. The effectiveness of the medications prescribed for those with diabetes and those who have blood-clotting problems can be monitored with these devices. When the values obtained by a patient are found to be abnormal, the results must be reported to a physician and are then verified by clinical laboratory testing. The use of these home clinical aids has increased. Current home testing devices include those to detect pregnancy, urine dipstick testing for glucose, and the prothrombin time (to assess blood clotting). Adding to this list are a male infertility test, an ovulation test kit, glucose determination by means of a hemoglobin component, and tests for some addictive drugs.

The Development of Kits That Aid in Diagnosis

Test kits developed by diagnostic companies are used by clinical laboratory scientists in medical laboratories. The kits have reagents with instructions for conducting the test and information on how to interpret test results. An example is found in the microbiology laboratory, where test kits are used as aids in identifying different species of the *Enterococci*, *Staphylococci*, and *Streptococci* pathogens. In these differential biochemical reaction kits, a portion of a bacterial culture grown in the laboratory is added to a system of chambers containing chemical solutions. These are usually the size of a pencil box. The little chambers are inoculated with a portion of the unknown bacterial culture. The bacteria are allowed to grow, and their biochemical and physical reactions help identify the one causing the infection in a patient.

Local Test Development

A test can also originate in a local clinical laboratory to fill a need in the surrounding population. For example, a chemical or a microbe may be causing a health problem in the community, so a test is needed to determine its source and to measure its impact. An example of this is a test to detect lead poisoning in children. The setting for this could be a city where old, loose house paint covers their play area. If lead is in the paint—then on the hands and in the mouths of children—serious illness can result.

For this type of analyte, a clinical laboratory may choose to use a test that is developed within its walls. We can be assured that these tests are reliable because the methodology is carefully and scientifically developed in a licensed or accredited clinical laboratory by scientists with years of experience. The developed procedure goes through a process of testing and validation to ensure that it measures the analyte accurately.

These laboratory-developed test procedures are carried out day after day in clinical laboratories. Included in this group are the Pap smears and manual cell counts on spinal fluid, on chest fluid, and on semen. Cultures grown in microbiology and tests for bacterial sensitivity to antibiotics are also included in this group. Blood bank compatibility testing for transfusions and the examination of tissue sections for pathological changes are also clinical laboratory–developed tests.

Public Safety and Reliable Testing

The public is guaranteed accuracy and precision in testing because all licensed and accredited clinical laboratories adhere to quality-assurance measures in order to qualify for licensure or accreditation. The term *quality assurance* refers to certain quality-control requirements that must be met, including national certification of laboratory personnel, the adherence to specific guidelines in all testing procedures, and participation in a proficiency testing program. The last is an internal examination of all aspects of the testing process by a state agency or a professional organization examining body. These requirements must be complied with so that a clinical laboratory can maintain licensure or accreditation.

Federal laws provide operational guidelines for clinical laboratories to follow. These laws were enacted after poor compliance with accepted standards of testing was reported for a few laboratories in large cities across the country. The enactments by Congress to halt this type of activity were the Clinical Laboratory Improvement Act, the Amendments of 1967 and 1988, and additional amendments currently being added. It is clear that as a health-care consumer using the services of these clinical laboratories, you can be assured that your test results are reliable. It is a good idea when using the services of a physician's office or commercial laboratory that you look for evidence of compliance with current laws by noticing licensure and other documents of this nature displayed on the walls.

DIFFERENT CLASSIFICATIONS FOR TESTS

Most clinical tests used for diagnostic purposes are performed on blood and urine. The US Food and Drug Administration approves and regulates these tests. State health departments throughout the country also have laws that regulate clinical laboratory testing performed within their jurisdiction.

The FDA has three categories for the approval of medical devices, which include some laboratory tests. Those tests that can "prevent human health from being impaired" are within the FDA Class III category. This group includes procedures to detect cancer and tests to detect certain viruses or the antibodies our bodies produce to fight them. Disorders in this category are considered hazards to our health, which, if allowed to cause disease, can be fatal. Class III tests require the FDA to review clinical research data collected by a manufacturer while the test was being developed.

Additional examples of Class III devices are the pacemaker implants for heart disease, breast implants, and molecular markers for cancer detection and for viral hepatitis. The Class III tests are the most complex and make up about 10 percent of the test volume for clinical laboratories. When a result is positive, it represents a risk of illness or injury to a patient. Therefore, the FDA wants to know all about these tests' development and trials.

Class I and Class II Tests

The Class I and II medical devices must show that there is no risk to the patient if there is an error in the procedure or in the interpretation of test results. In addition, the FDA has prior knowledge of these tests and of the equipment used in the procedures because similar tests already exist. If there is a new procedure that the agency is unfamiliar with, then a premarket approval (PMA) application must be submitted. This should give evidence of human clinical trials that show the effectiveness of the test for the purpose it was designed. Approximately half of the tests and medical devices are in the Class I category, which includes iron and cholesterol determinations and pregnancy tests.

Class II tests comprise a little less than half of the medical determinations and include most of the clinical chemistry and hematology (blood cell study) testing. Some examples are glucose determination, the hematocrit test, folic acid determination, the automated CBC, and the bilirubin and albumin tests.

COVERAGE OF CLINICAL TESTS

It is clear that the development of a clinical test is an arduous task that takes dedication by a number of people. After it is completed to the satisfaction of those who have developed it and to the FDA, another hurdle must be met. When a physician requests the test, will it be paid for by the patient's health insurance?

There is a complicated way in which the reimbursement for tests is determined. First, there is a current procedural terminology, called the CPT code, that is assigned to each clinical test. This is done by the American Medical Association (AMA), which publishes a CPT manual each year in which new tests are given a code, and any changes in the codes of established tests are found. The manual is used by health insurers to determine the reimbursement rates for medical tests and devices. The listings are extensive and can have as many as eight thousand codes. This manual can be found in a reference library.

Health Insurers

There are several types of insurers. A private insurer serves companies that provide their employees with health insurance plans. Insurers also serve private citizens who want health insurance at a reasonable rate. This rate is determined by the number of people in the group.

There are government insurers that you know as Medicare and Medicaid. Medicare takes care of payments for seniors, the elderly, and the disabled. Medicaid pays for services to those who are unable to pay for their health-care needs.

With regard to Medicare, the amount of reimbursement that will be paid and whether a clinical test is covered is important because the private insurers follow the policies of the agency in this regard. The standard used by Medicare for evaluating a procedure and paying for it is whether the test is reasonable and necessary for the diagnosis or treatment of an illness or injury. Unfortunately, this prohibits coverage of some clinical laboratory screening tests, which are described throughout this book and are used by physicians when a disease is suspected. These tests verify or negate the tentative diagnosis the doctor has made. The result of a screening test, if used correctly, allows for the early discovery of disease, which can save insurers money because the cost of treating a full-blown disease is much greater than trying to prevent the progress of an early one.

Local Medical Review Policies

Insurance companies that contract with Medicare for payment claims sometimes use what is called Local Medical Review Policies (LMRP), a mechanism for determining coverage policies for new types of tests. The payment is set by local providers in the community by consensus. As a result, a national laboratory could find that the same test submitted to a carrier for payment in different states is paid for in one and not in another.

Congress has found this to be undesirable and, as a result of a 1997 ruling, the Centers for Medicare and Medicaid Services (CMS) is required to review and improve policies regarding reimbursements for medical tests and devices. It is predicted that when this review is completed and national coverage decisions go into effect as a result of this legislation, about half of all tests submitted for reimbursement will be priced according to national standards. When this happens, individual tests will cost the same throughout the country.

For more information on this subject, these references are helpful: American Association for Clinical Chemistry Inc., "How Clinical Laboratory Tests Get to Market," *Lab Tests on Line* [online], http://www.labtestsonline.org, [February 2003]; College of American Pathologists, "CLIA Waived Test List," *CAP Laboratory Improvement-Surveys/Excel* [online], http://www .cap.org/html/lip [December 12, 2002].

chapter 2

Hematology

SECTION 1. THE BLOOD SYSTEM

Plain Facts

*H*ematology literally means the study of blood. When blood is sampled for testing, it is taken from veins on the inside of your arm by means of venipuncture. When a small amount is needed for a test, your fingertip or earlobe is pricked.

Your blood is a complex liquid. The liquid substance is plasma and suspended in it are cells and different organic products that come from the diet and our individual body chemistry. In order to be able to see the cells, a drop of blood is placed on a glass slide one by three inches in size. A smear is made by using another glass slide to form a thin film of blood. When dried and stained with special dyes, the nuclei and cytoplasm of the blood cells show up clearly when viewed with a microscope.

In its center, a cell has a nucleus made up of deoxyribonucleic acid (DNA). The nucleus is surrounded by cytoplasm, which contains many structures, most notably the various forms of ribonucleic acid (RNA). The nucleus takes part in cell division, and the RNA aids in the production of the protein product of each type of cell.

The Important Parts

The blood system is made up of several important parts. Two of these are the circulating blood and the bone marrow. Blood circulates through our veins and arteries. Blood cells are formed in the bone marrow, and when mature they are released into the circulation. Active bone marrow, where blood cells develop, is present in the sternum (chest bone), the hip bone, the lower spinal vertebrae, and bones of the arms and legs. When a sample of bone marrow is needed for a diagnosis, it can be removed from one of these locations.

Cells Are the Center of Attention

In the hematology laboratory, we are most concerned with blood cells. Each cell has a common name and a scientific name. For now we will use the common names. There are red blood cells (RBCs), white blood cells (WBCs), and platelets. Mature forms of these cells circulate in normal blood all the time.

When immature forms appear, this usually means that an infection or an anemia is present. These young cells have been released from the bone marrow before they are mature. Usually this is a rescue operation so that the body can maintain a healthy state in the face of threats. If, in addition to young cells, abnormal forms are present, the situation is more serious. Abnormal cells are characterized by unusual shapes, may be larger than normal, or have some structures called inclusions within them that do not belong there. This may signal the start of an infection, a type of anemia, a leukemia, or a lymphoma. These unusual cells may be a sign of a disorder that has been discovered at an early stage of development.

A Close-up Picture of Blood Cells: The White Blood Cell Differential Count

How do we observe these blood cells? The answer to this question is a test called the white blood cell differential count. It makes use of the blood smear referred to previously and is performed with the aid of a microscope. It is a part of the complete blood count (CBC), the most common laboratory test.

A differential count is a valuable tool for physicians because infections, anemias, and leukemias—in other words, cell abnormalities—are discovered here. During this count, white cells are placed into groups depending on the type of cell. The total number of each cell type that is seen is an important diagnostic tool. You will see why as you read on. The WBC differential count is described fully in the test section of this chapter.

SECTION 2. CELL TYPES

I. The White Blood Cells

The main cell types are white blood cells (leukocytes) and red blood cells. The former come in a variety of forms, and each has a different function. The main groups are granulocytes, lymphocytes, and monocytes. All of these cells have a nucleus with cytoplasm surrounding it. When looked at with a microscope, they have different sizes and colors. The sizes of white blood cells range from ten to fourteen microns in diameter.

The granulocytes are of three types. They are medium in size, and when stained with appropriate dyes, the majority of them—called neutrophils—have pink granules in the cytoplasm. There is an occasional granulocyte that has red granules, the eosinophil, and a rare one having purple granules, the basophil. Each type of granulocyte has an important function. The white blood cell that is most numerous when we examine a normal differential white cell count is the neutrophil. You will understand the reason for this when you learn their function.

As we look at the dyed blood smear, there are small WBCs called lymphocytes. They take on a medium blue color with a large dark blue nucleus, which fills up most of the cell. Monocytes are the largest cell in the circulating blood. They have a lot of grayish-blue cytoplasm with a large nucleus that has several folds resembling lobes. These cells have important functions, too.

What Are Some Tasks of WBCs?

There are two important functions of WBCs: (1) fighting infection and (2) building body immunity.

Fighting infection is performed by neutrophils and monocytes, the warriors of the body. They fight the enemy, which can be bacteria, viruses, or foreign bodies that have pierced the skin or invaded inner organs.

When you see abscesses, pimples, slivers, and so forth, the white material around the area affected is composed of white cells, the enemy, and dead material produced by the battle that has taken place. The granules in the white cells contain biochemicals and enzymes that are released when bacteria are surrounded by the cell. The invader is killed in this way.

If you have a chest cold or sinus infection, the yellow material coughed up or the nasal discharge is the same—WBCs, the enemy, and the dead material from the battle. If the battle is severe, the bone marrow pushes out more WBCs to win it. This is evidence of the body's reaction to the threat.

A "Shift to the Left"

When young WBCs show up among the mature ones on the differential white cell count, they are easily recognized. All of the different stages of cell development that take place in the bone marrow are seen in the circulating blood. This is a startling sight because these young forms are not usually seen in a normal smear. Their presence means that careful examination should follow so that more signs of a developing disorder are discovered.

Young WBCs' appearance indicates that stress has been put on the bone marrow due to an infection or a developing illness. The bone marrow's response is to release young cells before they are ready to act as adult cells. Physicians regard this "shift to the left" as a sign that the cause must be found by additional testing.

Serious Illness

During an illness, young cells are not the only ones appearing on a blood smear that should not be there. Abnormal forms may show up, too. Abnormal forms are structurally different, and, as with young cells, they do not perform the job they are supposed to in the body. A reason must be found for their presence, too.

The second function of WBCs is building body immunity. This is achieved by the lymphocytes, which build up our immune defense system. They are divided into two types, T-lymphocytes and B-lymphocytes.

The T-lymphocyte

T-lymphocytes are responsible for an immune response by means of cell activity. They can attack foreign elements in the blood directly. For example, an infection by disease-causing bacteria stimulates the bone marrow to produce more T-lymphocytes, which are programmed to destroy the invader. They are effective in protecting us against bacteria, fungi, and one-celled parasites, as well as some viruses. The entire cohort of T-lymphocytes that have met the enemy are programmed to destroy it.

The B-lymphocyte

The other immunity builders are the B-lymphocytes, which are also stimulated when an enemy invades the body. They are transformed into cells that produce and secrete antibodies called immunoglobulins (Igs), which are protein substances in the blood that protect us from infection. The immunoglobulins are natural vaccines produced by the body against invading pathogens. They have the same effect of destroying the enemy.

II. Red Blood Cells

The red blood cells are smaller than any of the white cells, but there are many more of them. When we examine a stained blood smear, they are the most numerous cell—the entire background is RBCs as we view the smear with a microscope. Their shape is that of a disc approximately seven microns in diameter. You might say they look like tiny red checkers. They contain hemoglobin, an iron-carrying compound that gives blood its red color.

The hemoglobin inside these cells is important because it takes up oxygen from the lungs as we inhale and carries it to the body tissues to be used for energy. We need energy at the cellular level to make our muscles contract. The exchange of oxygen and carbon dioxide in our lungs also requires energy. In fact, all body activity requires energy, including the absorption of nutrients by intestinal cells, the storage of sugar by liver cells, and the elimination of wastes by kidney cells. It is clear that hemoglobin is one of the most important biochemicals in our bodies. Therefore, a normal number of red blood cells is essential for good health and normal body function. If the number of these cells is low, an anemia is present, and the cause must be found.

III. Platelets

A platelet is the smallest particle in blood and not considered to be a cell. It is much smaller than a red cell—so small that it is barely visible on a dye-stained blood smear. Platelets usually appear in little clumps on the stained blood smear, which allows us to see them more readily than if they remained alone. The main function of platelets is to maintain normal blood clotting. If they do their job, no excess blood is lost when a small blood vessel is ruptured by a cut. (There is more information about platelets in the chapter on coagulation.)

IV. How Many Is Normal?
The Reference Range or Normal Range

When you look at the laboratory report provided by your physician, the numbers that appear on the right provide a range of normal values for each test. This is actually the normal numerical range for the substance we are measuring. These values for each analyte have been determined by clinical laboratory scientists for a group of people in a certain locality who are healthy. It is also called a reference range.

The reference range for a red cell count is 4.2 million to 5.9 million cells in each microliter of blood. A microliter is one millionth of a liter and amounts to a drop from an eyedropper.

The reference range for a white cell count is five thousand to ten thousand cells in each microliter of blood. Children normally have a slightly higher white cell count than adults to stave off infections.

V. The First Sign of a Blood Disorder

An anemia is present with most disorders of the blood and is a symptom of a developing illness. The underlying cause of the anemia must be discovered by further tests. When an anemia is present, red cells change in size and shape as well as decrease in number.

There are many types of anemias. The way a clinical scientist keeps track is to classify them according to simple observations of the RBCs, such as changes in their size, shape, and degree of redness. For example, if the red cell is pale, then there is less hemoglobin than normal. Red blood cells can be classified by these observations so that the exact type of anemia can be found. You will understand this better as you read on.

Sizing Up Red Blood Cells: Their Shape and Volume

The following description is a method of determining the type of anemia a patient is suffering from. The size, shape, and amount of redness of the RBCs are expressed in numbers or measurements. This system or classification is very useful to a physician, and you will see why. The measurements that result from certain hematology tests are inserted into equations to calculate what we call red blood cell indexes. The indexes give us an answer as to what kind of anemia is the culprit and a clue of the underlying disorder, both of which are confirmed by further tests.

When automated cell counters are used, some of these indexes are measured directly. The equations for determining them are described here to give you a better understanding of their meaning in terms of red cell morphology (or form).

The red cell indexes are included in the automated complete blood count test report. They are the MCV, MCH, and MCHC and can be verified by a clinical laboratory scientist when she examines the stained blood smear of the differential white cell count.

The red cell indexes are described here. The word *cell* is substituted for corpuscular in the following descriptions.

The Mean Corpuscular (Cell) Volume (MCV)

This is a measurement of red blood cell size. When the index is calculated, the test values used in the equation are the red cell count and the hematocrit—a test that measures the space in the circulating blood stream occupied by red cells. (A description of the hematocrit is in the test section of this chapter.) A lower-than-normal MCV is demonstrated by the appearance of small RBCs. A high MCV means larger-than-normal red cells.

The Mean Cell Hemoglobin (MCH)

The MCH is a measurement of the color or amount of hemoglobin in each red blood cell. When the index is calculated, the test values used in the equation are the hemoglobin and red cell count. Cells having a low MCH are called hypochromic. The "chromic" refers to color, and "hypo" means less color than normal. Therefore, these red cells have less color and, of course, less hemoglobin. When cells have normal red color, they are normochromic.

The Mean Cell Hemoglobin Concentration (MCHC)

This is an indicator of the amount of hemoglobin in circulating red blood cells regardless of the size of each red cell. When this index is calculated, the test values used in the equation are the hemoglobin and the hematocrit. The MCHC measures the amount of hemoglobin in a certain volume of blood without regard to red cell size and form.

Currently in most clinical laboratories, the indexes are provided by an automated cell counter.

The Red Cell Distribution Width (RDW)

This is a measurement provided by some automated hematology instruments that shows the distibution of cell volume among the red blood cells. It indicates the variation in size of the RBCs if they were viewed in a peripheral blood smear. The reference range is 12.2 to 14.6 percent.

VI. The Telltale Signs

The red blood cell's size, shape, and depth of color are important for the clinical scientist to observe because descriptions of anemias are in these real terms. A numerical description like the RBC indexes helps us to understand the type of disease that is present in a patient. With this information, physicians have a diagnosis, and effective treatment can be started.

A Classification of Anemias

The names used here to describe the red cells and the different shapes they take on in disease are in the form of a classification. There are various ways of classifying the types of anemias. This one is based on the red blood cell indexes that have been described.

The First Group

When a disorder is detected and the red cells are normal in size (normocytic) and color (normochromic), there could be a problem with blood cell formation in the bone marrow. Another cause of this type of anemia is the presence of tumor cells in the bone marrow. Although the red cells are normal in size and color, the red cell count is low. We see this in a variety of conditions, such as:

- uncomplicated infectious mononucleosis
- chronic infections
- inflammatory conditions such as rheumatoid arthritis
- chronic tuberculosis
- chronic kidney disease
- disorders of the endocrine system (which includes the pituitary [master gland], the thyroid, the parathyroid, the insulin-producing cells of the pancreas, the adrenal glands located on each kidney. Disorders occur when these glands produce too much or too little secretion)
- malignant conditions when tumor cells invade the bone marrow.

Within this group, there may also be some RBCs that show abnormal shapes. The content of hemoglobin is normal with good red color, but some of the RBCs are not in the normal disc shape. The RBC indexes are within the normal range, even though there are some abnormal shapes that give us a clue to the type of anemia that is present and a cause of the disorder. This blood cell picture can be seen in

- sickle cell anemia,
- severe kidney disease,
- carcinoma of the bone marrow, and
- certain stages of leukemia.

The Second Group

When the red cells are larger than normal in diameter (macrocytic) and normal in color (normochromic), there is a possibility of a vitamin B_{12} or folic acid deficiency. A liver disorder can also cause a macrocytic, normochromic anemia.

Because of the larger diameter, there is a high MCV index. A cause of the anemia is a destruction of the macrocytes as they pass through the tiny passages of the spleen. The red cell count, the hemoglobin, and the hematocrit are decreased because some of the RBCs are being destroyed. This type of anemia can be seen in

- chronic liver disease
- diminshed thyroid activity (hypothyroidism)
- vitamin B_{12} or folic acid deficiencies (additional testing is performed to determine which deficiency is causing the abnormal cell population because treatment for each is different)
- pernicious anemia
- alcoholism
- an interaction of various drugs
- some types of birth control medications
- gastrectomy (surgery of the stomach)
- tapeworm infection
- chemotherapy treatment.

The Third Group

When the red cells are smaller than normal and do not have enough hemoglobin, they are microcytic and hypochromic. The red cell indexes are all low, reflecting a decreased red blood cell count and a low hemoglobin value.

Some of the factors that can cause this type of disorder are

- not enough iron in the diet
- a chronic loss of blood
- thalassemia (Mediterranean anemia), a hereditary illness
- iron being consumed but not fully used by the bone marrow to produce red cells.

Normal and abnormal red blood cells magnified more than 1500 times the normal size

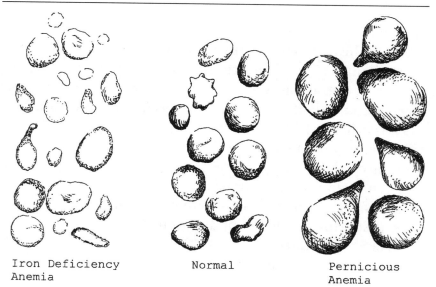

Iron Deficiency
Anemia

Normal

Pernicious
Anemia

SECTION 3. SOME TESTS PERFORMED IN A HEMATOLOGY LABORATORY

Introduction

Clinical laboratory scientists in a hematology laboratory currently use automated instruments for counting red blood cells and white blood cells and for the differential white blood cell count. The manual CBC is not as widely used today. However, the microscopic examination of a dye-stained blood smear to perform the differential white cell count is still valuable to a physician in certain illnesses. It reveals distinctive abnormalities of red and white blood cells when anemias and leukemias are present. It also aids in identifying infections such as infectious mononucleosis and parasitic infestations. In addition, a report of the differential count helps a physician in monitoring a patient's progress and his or her response to therapy.

A limited white blood cell differential count may be done in the physician's office laboratory on a small, recently developed instrument that is not much larger than a bread box. When this test shows abnormal results, it is repeated in a clinical laboratory to verify them.

Screening Tests

There are some tests that are considered "screening tests." They explore certain factors that the physician suspects are causing the patient's symptoms. These tests are important preliminary assessments of a body system that could be causing a patient some distress. They may be tests to discover an anemia or to find early diabetes.

When a physician finds that a physical examination and a family history of disorders does not provide an answer to a patient's complaints, a screening test is used. If the test is positive, further testing is necessary to find the deeper cause of the problem.

A good example of a screening test is the complete blood count used to discover anemias and much more. You will find as you read on that a CBC provides valuable information to the health-care team.

The Clinical Tests

The following are tests performed by clinical laboratory scientists in a hematology laboratory. Disorders mentioned here are briefly described in the disease section of the chapter.

Body Fluid Examination

Body fluid is examined to look for different types of cells. When cells that belong in the circulating blood are found in other areas of the body, the cause must be investigated. In normal circumstances, these areas of the body should be sterile with no blood cells in them, so valuable information is gained when these cells and evidence of inflammation are found. This escaped blood could be present in cerebrospinal fluid, joint fluid, abdominal fluid, or chest fluid. The cells are present as a result of an illness or a malignancy in which blood vessels become leaky, and inflammatory cells—as well as blood cells—appear in these fluids. Large protein molecules and certain tissue cells are also present.

A physician obtains a sample of the fluid from a joint, the

chest cavity, the spinal column, or anywhere blood cells could be waging the battle of resistance. The fluid is sampled by withdrawing it with a needle and syringe, then it is examined by a clinical scientist for blood and tumor cells. A pathologist may also examine it for tumor cells.

Bone Marrow Examination

This procedure is performed by a physician who is usually a hematologist. A CBC screening test has revealed some unusual findings, and a bone marrow aspiration is indicated. For a bone marrow aspiration, the sternum (chest bone) and the posterior iliac crest (hip bone) are most often tapped to obtain liquid marrow.

Several smears are made of the liquid marrow and of the tiny particles in it. They are stained with the same dyes used for blood smears because these dyes reveal important characteristics of blood cells that help to identify them. After the staining process, there is a microscopic examination of all the prepared slides to identify and classify the cells present.

This classification helps to determine the cell line of origin, namely, granulocytes, lymphocytes, red blood cells, or monocytes. The maturity and any abnormal characteristics that cells may have are noted. After careful examination of all the bone marrow slides, it is usually possible for a hematologist or pathologist to make a diagnosis of the blood disorder the patient is suffering from.

The results of the bone marrow aspiration are often correlated with a bone marrow biopsy, taken at the same time. The biopsy is an actual sliver of bone marrow tissue and some of the surrounding bone. By examining the biopsy, a pathologist is able to see the number of cells that are being produced by a patient—either fewer cells than normal or more than the normal number. The pathologist or hematologist also observes any pattern of abnormal cells that has developed. All of these factors help to arrive at an accurate diagnosis.

Complete Blood Count (CBC)

The CBC and urinalysis tests are among the most useful screening tests for medical diagnoses. The CBC, an automated test for detecting anemias, leukemias, infections, and many other disorders, requires a small test tube of blood that is not clotted. The red blood cells and white blood cells are counted. The differential white blood cell count is performed.

The automated CBC also includes a hemoglobin determination, a hematocrit, and a platelet count. The red cell indexes that have been discussed—namely, the MCV, MCH, and MCHC—are also provided. More information about the automated cell counter can be found in the glossary.

Differential White Blood Cell Count

This test is part of the automated CBC. However, if manual examination of the blood smears by a clinical laboratory scientist is needed, smears are made. A drop of the anticoagulated (nonclotted) blood is placed on a glass slide, then spread into a thin film with another slide. Usually two of them are prepared for each patient. They are gently dried and then stained with a series of dyes to show clearly the nucleus, cytoplasm, and internal structures of each cell when viewed with a microscope.

**Examining the Cells in a Differential
White Cell Count**

During this procedure, whether performed by an automated cell counter or manually, white blood cells are classified as granulocytes, monocytes, and lymphocytes. The granulocytes outnumber the other WBCs when they are fighting an enemy invader.

When you look at your clinical laboratory report, the percentage of each type of white blood cell, the indexes, and a brief description of red cell morphology (form) can be found when a CBC is requested. When the test results are not within the reference ranges, a clinical laboratory scientist examines the smears with a microscope to observe all of the cells for abnormal forms.

Hemoglobin Electrophoresis

There are several clinical laboratory tests in which electrophoresis is used, and one performed in a clinical chemistry laboratory measures proteins in the blood. Another, a hematology test, is used to identify normal and abnormal forms of hemoglobin that may be causing a disorder in a patient. During this test, hemoglobin molecules move in an electric field on a band of cellulose acetate, which is the support medium for the blood sample. Different types of hemoglobin display different rates of movement on this medium. The percentages of normal hemoglobins are hemoglobin A, 95 percent; hemoglobin A_2, 2–4 percent; and fetal hemoglobin, less than 2 percent. When abnormal forms or amounts are found, such as those in the disorders thalassemia and sickle cell anemia, the diagnosis is complete. A type of treatment can be started.

Hematocrit

This test, provided by the automated CBC, measures the space taken up by blood cells in a given volume of blood that is not allowed to clot. The hematocrit represents the volume of blood cells suspended in plasma in the individual's circulating blood. This test can also be performed manually by using a test tube, called a microhematocrit tube, made especially for the test.

In the test, a fine, capillary-size glass tube is filled with anticoagulated blood. A special centrifuge spins the tubes at a certain speed for a specified time. Then, the volume of packed red blood cells in the bottom half of the test tube is measured. This portion of the tube is red, while the top half contains straw-colored plasma. A fine line of white is seen between the two. These are the white blood cells. This observation proves that red cells greatly outnumber white cells in the circulating blood.

The reference values for a hematocrit are 37 percent to 47 percent for women and 42 percent to 52 percent for men. When this test result is too low, the physician has evidence of the presence and severity of an anemia.

Hemoglobin Determination

This test is part of the automated CBC. Hemoglobin is contained in the red blood cells. The reference range for women is twelve to sixteen grams in a deciliter of blood and for men, fourteen to eighteen grams in a deciliter.

Platelet Count

This test gives us the number of platelets, the smallest particles in blood, present in a microliter of blood. The count can be performed manually, but an automated cell counter provides it as part of the CBC. The reference range for platelets is one hundred fifty thousand to four hundred fifty thousand in each microliter.

Red Blood Cell Count

This automated count of the RBCs in a microliter of blood is part of the CBC. A normal number of red cells, 4.2 million to 5.9 million in each microliter of blood, is essential for good health.

White Blood Cell Count

This is an automated count of the WBCs (leukocytes) in a sample of blood. These cells are larger than red blood cells, but there are fewer of them. The reference range is five thousand to ten thousand in each microliter of blood.

SECTION 4. DISEASES OF THE BLOOD SYSTEM

Introduction

In this section, diseases that involve the blood system are discussed in alphabetical order. The most common one that all of us are susceptible to on a daily basis is infection. This happens most often when we are victims of the common cold, a sore throat, or an earache.

Other disorders discussed here happen often enough so that you will benefit from knowing something about them. Serious diseases that occur when both blood and bone marrow are under a great amount of stress are also described.

Aplastic Anemia

In this anemia, the red blood cells are decreased in number but appear to have normal shape. A reason for the decrease is that fewer of them are being produced in the bone marrow. This type of anemia can be inherited or acquired. Some of the ways it is acquired are through

- exposure to certain chemicals or drugs
- exposure to radiation
- severe infections
- the early stages of leukemia.

This disorder is treated with red blood cell transfusions. When necessary, platelet transfusions are provided to prevent bleeding episodes. Antibiotics are prescribed to minimize infections. Another form of treatment is the bone marrow transplant.

Autoimmune Hemolytic Anemia

This disorder is caused by an abnormality in the immune system. Certain cells in the body are not recognized as the patient's own. The result is that antibodies are formed against them, a condition known as autoimmunity. When the immune reaction is directed against the person's red blood cells, they are injured by the antibodies and eventually destroyed. When these red cells burst, they are no longer functional, and the anemia results. Hemoglobin has been released into the bloodstream. The term for this destruction of the red cells is *hemolysis*, and the type of anemia is *hemolytic*.

An autoimmune hemolytic anemia may occur in various conditions, including when a patient has a viral infection, in the presence of a malignant tumor, or when a patient has systemic lupus erythematosus (an autoimmune disorder). The treatment for the anemia varies with the cause.

Bacterial Infections

When you are a victim of a bacterial infection, the number of white blood cells increases. This is because the bone marrow releases more than the usual number to fight the invading bacteria. There are also young, immature white blood cells.

Our defense against bacterial invasion is provided by the neutrophils that live in blood and in tissues. They surround and consume the bacteria that attack the tissue. These infections commonly occur in the throat, lungs, or skin.

A white cell differential count (part of the CBC) reveals signs of bacterial invasion by the large number of neutrophils and the presence of young cell forms that do not belong in the bloodstream. You know from your previous reading that this means a "left shift" of this cell type.

When physical findings suggest a serious infection, the physician uses this information as a sign that appendicitis, peritonitis, or diverticulitis may be present in a patient.

Folic Acid Deficiency

When you eat green, leafy vegetables or liver and other meats or certain fruits, your folic acid stores are satisfied. The cause of a deficiency may be (1) a diet low in these foods or (2) the vitamins and minerals that are eaten are not being absorbed by the lining cells of the small intestine, where nutrients enter the bloodstream.

When there is a pronounced deficiency of folic acid, a macrocytic anemia results. You may recall that the cells of this anemia are larger than normal. Young, immature, and abnormal RBCs are being released into the circulating blood. The differential white blood cell count shows the macrocytes, some of them in unusual teardrop and oval shapes, and abnormal white blood cells. In this anemia, WBCs and platelets are decreased in number and so is the hemoglobin.

Tests that help in the diagnosis of a folic acid deficiency include the

- complete blood count
- folic acid blood levels
- bone marrow examination, as indicated by the other test results.

Hemolytic Anemia

This is a group of anemias in which red blood cells do not survive their normal life span because they have defects of various kinds. As these defective RBCs pass through blood and lymph vessels of the spleen, they are destroyed. The passageways through spleen tissue are narrow. Normal RBCs can survive this trial, but defective ones cannot. Several conditions cause these malformed RBCs to appear. For example, some red cells contain abnormal hemoglobin, and others have cell wall (membrane) abnormalities. Another cause of this type of anemia in some people is the effect of chemical and physical agents from the environment.

When red cells burst, they release hemoglobin. As a result of biochemical activity in the body, hemoglobin is changed to bilirubin, a form of bile. An excess of this product in the bloodstream may turn the skin yellow. Another result of hemolysis is an enlarged spleen. There is evidence of this when a biopsy of the organ is examined with a microscope and reveals it is packed with red cell fragments. Sometimes the spleen is removed surgically as a form of treatment to minimize red blood cell destruction. These are some of the problems that can occur when a patient has a long-standing hemolytic anemia.

Hodgkin's Lymphoma

This is a disorder of the lymphoid tissue of the spleen and lymph nodes. The lymphatic system carries lymph, a fluid that generally has WBCs but no RBCs, throughout the body in vessels similar to our veins. Lymphocytes, formed in lymphoid tissue, are involved in this disorder. Eventually, the lymph traveling through the lymph vessels is added to the blood circulation. You may recall that one of the functions of lymphocytes is to provide cells with the ablility to fight invaders. This function is compromised when Hodgkin's is present.

Hodgkin's occurs in young and middle-aged people. A CBC reveals an anemia with normocytic, hypochromic red blood cells. An excess production of gamma immunoglobulins— which are discussed in chapter 6—occurs in this disorder. This is seen with the serum electrophoresis test.

Diagnosis

A diagnosis is made by obtaining a biopsy of tissue from an enlarged lymph node. A pathologist confirms the diagnosis and classifies it by examining a paper-thin slice of the lymph node with a microscope. Certain cellular patterns help classify the type of Hodgkin's present. Finding a particular cell called the Reed-Sternberg is also important. The cell is large compared with those surrounding it and has several nuclei. When it is found, a diagnosis of Hodgkin's lymphoma can be made.

This disorder is curable today by a combination of drugs, radiation therapy, and chemotherapy.

You may have heard the term *lymphoma*, a general name that refers to various disorders in which the lymphoid tissue proliferates abnormally. Other types of lymphomas exist but are not discussed in this book.

Infectious Mononucleosis

This is an acute, benign infection of lymph tissue caused by the Epstein-Barr virus.

Onset of the illness is accompanied by a fever, a sore throat, and an accumulation of pus. The physician's examination reveals enlarged lymph nodes, especially in the neck, armpit, and groin. The differential white cell count shows both an increase in lymphocytes and, most importantly, a specific type of abnormal cell called an atypical lymphocyte. When these lymphocytes are seen accompanied by the characteristic clinical symptoms, a diagnosis of infectious mononucleosis (IM) can be made.

The heterophile antibody test is also diagnostic, but it becomes positive after the appearance of the abnormal lymphocytes. When a patient has recovered, a CBC test is valuable again to show a decrease in the abnormal lymphocytes seen earlier in the illness. A patient with IM requires bedrest and normal nutrition, and complete recovery occurs in two months. There is a slow return of normal cells as the stained blood smear is examined at intervals during the patient's recovery.

Leukemia

This is a disease in which excess white blood cells are produced, resulting in an increased count. Both abnormal and immature cells appear in the circulating blood. By abnormal forms, I mean that they are structurally different, and they do not perform the job they are supposed to. There are small numbers of these forms at first, but as the illness progresses, the abnormal cells increase in number.

The causes of leukemia vary and include exposure to radiation, toxic chemicals, and some types of drugs. It is thought that exposure to some viruses can also cause leukemia. There is an inherited tendency in the case of some leukemias. They are classified as chronic or acute according to the maturity of the cells that predominate. The more common types of leukemia are

- myelogenous, in which the majority of cells are neutrophils;

- lymphocytic, in which lymphocytes predominate; and
- monocytic, where monocytes are prominent.

A CBC is the test in which a leukemia is discovered, but a bone marrow aspiration confirms the diagnosis. This test allows a physician hematologist or pathologist to make a prediction (prognosis) about the severity of the illness. Bone marrow aspiration is described in the test section of this chapter.

Fortunately, many types of leukemia can be cured today thanks to advances in treatment, including chemotherapy to reduce abnormal cell populations, radiation therapy, and bone marrow transplants.

Lymphopenia

The last part of this word, *penia*, means lesser, and in cell terms, it means a decrease in cell numbers. Therefore, in this condition a decrease in the number of lymphocytes is seen in the circulating blood when examining a stained blood smear. Some causes of this may be exposure to toxic substances, including chemicals and certain types of drugs, or viral infections.

It is interesting to note that a lymphopenia and leukopenia (a decrease in all WBCs, including granulocytes and monocytes) are among the first findings in infectious mononucleosis, which serves as a clue in IM's diagnosis. The lymphopenia and leukopenia are discovered in the differential white cell count of the CBC and the automated cell counts.

Malabsorption

In this disorder, nurtients are not being absorbed in the small intestine for different physiological reasons. There are different forms of this condition, but basically, nutrients from food do not move from the small intestine into the blood to be distributed throughout the body. One of the disorders that causes this is Crohn's disease, a chronic inflammation of the small intestine that prevents nutrients from being absorbed.

Another disorder of this type is Celiac disease, which is an irritation of the lining of the intestine (the mucosa) caused by gluten sensitivity, an allergy to the glycoprotein gluten found in wheat and other cereal grains. The allergy results in damage to the lining cells so that they cannot function properly.

A third disorder causing inflammation of the bowel is ulcerative colitis, a chronic irritation of the colon, with ulcerations that cause diarrhea and the appearance of blood in the stool.

These disorders are diagnosed by means of the following tests.

Screening procedures for nutritional deficiencies and malabsorption are the CBC and clinical chemistry tests such as serum albumin, phosphorus, calcium, and cholesterol determinations. A coagulation test, which measures how quickly the blood clots, called the prothrombin time is used. If the CBC is abnormal, a follow-up study of serum iron, vitamin B_{12}, and folic acid is performed.

Some conditions that could result from malabsorption are an anemia, low serum values for the protein albumin, vitamin deficiencies, and hidden (occult) blood being passed in the stool.

In gluten sensitivity (Celiac disease), the level of gliadin antibodies in the serum is determined. Gliadin is a fractional protein of gluten in wheat. A final test is a biopsy of the intestine, which is examined by a pathologist for cellular and tissue damage.

Other possible causes for test results and symptoms of this kind are parasitic infections and food poisoning. These must be eliminated before a final diagnosis of malabsorption is made.

These are just a few causes of malabsorption. A physician must carefully and tirelessly consider the array of symptoms and the test results to arrive at this difficult diagnosis.

Neutropenia

In this disorder, there is a decreased number of neutrophils. You may recall that these are the granulocytes that make up the majority of white blood cells. Some causes of a neutropenia can be

- a hereditary disorder in which the neutrophil count is consistently low,
- exposure to toxic substances, or
- viral infections.

A CBC discovers a neutropenia. The problem is that there are not enough neutrophils to defeat any bacteria that may invade the body. Additional tests are necessary to discover the cause of a neutropenia.

Sickle Cell Anemia

This is a hemolytic anemia in which the abnormal hemoglobin S is present in the RBCs. The S is for sickle, which is the shape taken on by some of the RBCs in this disorder. It occurs mainly in people of central African, North American, and Middle Eastern descent. Different amounts of hemoglobin S are present inside the cells, depending on the individual's hereditary genes. It follows that the amount of hemoglobin S inside the RBCs determines the severity of the anemia.

The scientific story behind the shape of these red cells is interesting. When there is a decreased amount of available oxygen in the blood, hemoglobin S forms long, thin crystals inside the RBCs. This event is called "sickling." The sickling process distorts the pliable outer membrane of the red cell, and it takes on the shape of the crystal.

When examining a stained blood smear with a microscope, occasional elongated and curved red cells with pointed ends are seen. These cells do not move in the blood circulation as well as the normal disc-shaped RBCs do. In fact, they make the blood less fluid and slow down the circulation. As a result, the blood flow in small blood vessels is sluggish, so less oxygen is carried to the organs and tissues.

These events lead to painful crises of the circulatory system, which affect the limbs and sometimes the organs of the patient. Crises signal that blood vessels have been closed off.

The test used to make this diagnosis is a CBC in which the differential white cell count shows an occasional sickle cell or the presence of red cell fragments that have been torn from the cells in the hemolytic process. Immature red cells and young white cells are seen, demonstrating a "left shift." These changes show that the bone marrow has increased the production of WBCs and RBCs to compensate for those being destroyed.

A Test to Bring on Sickling

Sickle cells may not show up on the stained blood smear, so it becomes questionable whether they are present, even though symptoms of the patient and other test results indicate that they are. A special test that causes sickle cells to form is performed. A mixture of certain chemicals and the patient's blood is prepared, which results in an oxygen-deprived environment on a glass slide. This causes the abnormal hemoglobin S to form visible crystals and distort the red cells, which can be seen when examined with a microscope. This test is positive only when hemoglobin S is present in the RBCs.

When we perform a hemoglobin electrophoresis, the test results show the different forms of hemoglobin in the patient's red cells. The abnormal hemoglobin S is observed and measured.

Treatment involves various drugs. A physician chooses the treatment after considering the severity of the anemia and the condition of a patient. The task is to ease the sickle cell crises, carry on exchange transfusions, and prevent infections.

Sickle Cell Trait

This is a less serious form of hemoglobin S disease. The blood of individuals with the "trait" contains some of the abnormal hemoglobin, but this small amount does not cause painful crises. Most of their blood is normal and functions well to carry oxygen to the tissues. Usually, there is no anemia, and the individual is able to live a normal life.

Systemic Lupus Erythematosus (SLE)

In this disorder of the immune system, the body produces antibodies against its own cells. It is an autoimmune disorder. The antibody that results from this reaction is called an autoantibody.

Most of us have immune systems that recognize "self," so our bodies do not ordinarily act against our own cells. Some of the factors that may bring on this disorder include changes in the tissues caused by an exposure to a virus or to certain chemicals, a defect in the way the body regulates the immune system, or a genetic alteration of the immune system.

In the CBC, there is evidence of a hemolytic anemia with a decreased number of granulocytes and platelets. An unusual cell called an "LE cell," found when examining the stained blood smear, is evidence of the antibody activity.

The autoantibodies attack target cells, injuring or killing them. There are a variety of symptoms, and a visible one is reddish skin lesions that sometimes form a butterfly shape over the bridge of the nose. In long-standing cases, there is inflammation of the blood vessels. This may lead to a rheumatoid condition with joint pain or to inflammation of the kidneys. As the disorder continues, a urinalysis test reveals an increase in protein due to damage of the glomeruli of the kidneys. Glomeruli are part of the nephron, the microscopic functional unit of the kidney. Approximately one million nephrons are in each kidney.

Treatment involves the use of nonsteroid anti-inflammatory drugs.

The LE Cell

Some of the autoantibodies may be directed against the nucleus of cells. When this happens, a combination of the antibody and target cell nucleus is formed, which causes the cell to malfunction and die. This is the result of an LE plasma factor present in the blood and body fluids that acts as an antinuclear autoantibody. The LE plasma factor attacks the cell's DNA (in the nucleus), and it becomes a globular mass. Then, neutrophils surround and engulf the dead cell. At this point, it is an LE cell.

The LE plasma factor can be detected by serologic tests such as immunofluorescense and radioimmunoassay, which are discussed in chapter 6. Some of the tests for this disorder are the

- CBC
- antinuclear antibody test
- immunoelectrophoresis to detect an increase in immunoglobins
- stained blood smear to detect the presence of LE cells.

Thalassemia (Mediterranean Anemia)

This anemia was thought to occur in people who lived in the area of the Mediterranean Sea. It is now believed that thalassemia occurs worldwide.

In this hemolytic anemia caused by a defect of hemoglobin, the individual's hereditary genes cause abnormal variations of hemoglobin. The severity of the disorder depends upon the types and amounts of abnormal hemoglobin present in the red cells.

Some of the hemoglobin combinations are unable to carry enough oxygen for normal body metabolism to occur. When serious variations are present in the red blood cells, the anemia may be severe enough to require regular transfusions. But when the deviation from normal hemoglobin is small, a mild anemia results, and good nutrition keeps the person healthy.

In the severe cases, the type of anemia is microcytic and hypochromic, and red blood cell destruction occurs. Slight jaundice may be visible in the skin. When the illness is prolonged, the spleen may be enlarged because the faulty red blood cells are being destroyed.

A diagnosis is made by means of the CBC and especially the differential white blood cell count. A hemoglobin electrophoresis test identifies the types of abnormal hemoglobin and the amounts of each.

Treatment for the severe form of this anemia is blood transfusions, but a diet of good nutrition is sufficient treatment for the mild form.

Viral Infections

Viral infections can occur in any organ of the body. In the respiratory system, they can cause pneumonia; in the liver, hepatitis; in the immune system, acquired immunodeficiency syndrome (AIDS); and in brain tissue, encephalitis.

When viruses have infected us, the CBC test results show a decrease in the number of neutrophils and an increase in the number of lymphocytes. This is the reverse of a bacterial infection, in which the neutrophils are increased in number. The lymphocytes that we see in the differential white blood cell count are activated ones typical for this condition. The patient's symptoms and evidence obtained from the CBC point to a virus infection. Further testing is performed to find the type of infecting virus. For example, there are molecular biotechnology tests for the viral diseases AIDS and hepatitis.

Vitamin B$_{12}$ Deficiency

This vitamin is found in dairy products, eggs, meat, and liver. The cause of a deficiency is rarely due to diet, but diet can be a factor in people who are strict vegetarians.

The most common cause is a failure of the stomach lining to secrete a substance that is necessary for vitamin B$_{12}$ to be absorbed by the cells of the small intestine. A manifestation of this problem is pernicious anemia, a hereditary disease that usually occurs after age forty.

A second cause for a deficiency of vitamin B$_{12}$ is an autoimmune disorder.

A third condition that brings on a deficiency has to do with the intestinal tract, which might fail to absorb nutrients that include vitamin B$_{12}$. This disorder is called malabsorption, an inadequate transfer of nutrients from the small intestine to the blood so that the body can use them.

A deficiency of this vitamin results in a macrocytic anemia with larger-than-normal RBCs. Vitamin B$_{12}$ is needed by the bone marrow to produce normal RBCs and WBCs. When there is not enough of this vitamin, the bone marrow releases young RBCs before they are mature to compensate. White blood cells and platelets are decreased as well as the hemoglobin. Some white blood cells show abnormal characteristics.

Vitamin B$_{12}$ administration is the treatment needed to restore normal bone marrow.

A Similar Blood Picture: Pernicious Anemia

If pernicious anemia is the suspected cause of a macrocytic anemia, it must be diagnosed by further tests. In this disorder, vitamin B_{12} is consumed but not absorbed. In advanced stages of the disease, there is central nervous system involvement in addition to gastrointestinal distress. When stomach secretions are analyzed, it is found that these patients have a decreased amount of a substance necessary for vitamin B_{12} absorption.

It has recently been found that individuals with pernicious anemia produce autoantibodies against specialized cells in the stomach, causing them to secrete a decreased amount of the substance needed for normal blood cell production.

Tests that help distinguish between vitamin B_{12} deficiency, pernicious anemia, and malabsorption are

- CBC
- stomach secretion analysis
- serum vitamin B_{12} blood levels (to detect a deficiency)
- bone marrow examination as indicated by other test results
- autoantibody test.

Additional information can be obtained in Barbara A. Brown, *Hematology: Principles and Procedures* (Philadelphia: Lea & Febinger, 1993); Denise M. Harmening, *Clinical Hematology and Fundamentals of Hemostasis* (Philadelphia: F. A. Davis, 1997).

chapter 3

Coagulation—
Blood Clotting

SECTION 1. THE COAGULATION SYSTEM

The Way It Works

When we sustain a wound or a fracture, a nearby blood vessel wall is opened and blood escapes into the surrounding tissues or to the outside of the body in case of external injury. The blood flow must be stopped, which is accomplished when blood clots. Another word for the clotting process is *coagulation*. Some body tissue substances and certain factors within our blood cause this to happen.

If we were looking at the injury through a microscope, we would see that the deep tissue layers of the injured blood vessel wall are exposed. At the same time, platelets from our bloodstream adhere to the damaged wall. The tissue of the vessel wall releases a factor that causes platelets to stick to each other, or aggregate, which plugs the opening and stops blood from escaping. At the same time, clotting proteins called coag-

73

ulation factors in the blood help stop the bleeding. The two elements, platelets and blood-clotting factors, interact with each other to convert one of the final products of this activity, prothrombin, into an enzyme called thrombin.

Thrombin then acts upon a circulating blood protein called fibrinogen. This reaction converts fibrinogen into fibrin, which is the main part of a clot. Fibrin is like a matrix on which the blood platelets and blood-clotting factors form the clot.

If the injury is extensive, this may take some time. Blood will clot from a small wound in two to eight minutes. However, when blood continues to flow, the wound may be closed with sutures by a physician. This helps to slow the blood flow and facilitate clot formation.

This is a simplified version of the coagulation cascade. All the factors must be activated by the previous one, so the term *cascade* is used. The result is the formation of a stable blood clot. Anywhere on this pathway there may be defects in clot formation. It is the responsibility of a clinical laboratory scientist to find the defect by testing.

A deficiency of any of the factors prolongs the time required to form a clot.

Coagulation Cascade

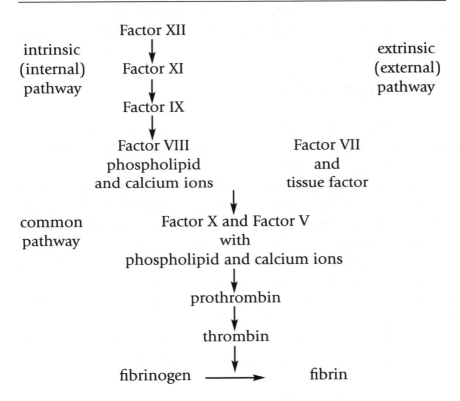

Factor XII

intrinsic
(internal)
pathway

Factor XI

extrinsic
(external)
pathway

Factor IX

Factor VIII
phospholipid
and calcium ions

Factor VII
and
tissue factor

common
pathway

Factor X and Factor V
with
phospholipid and calcium ions

prothrombin

thrombin

fibrinogen ⟶ fibrin

A Closer Look

The coagulation factors are represented by roman numerals and are divided into those of the intrinsic pathway and extrinsic pathway. As you look at the cascade, the intrinsic factors (on the left side) are those in the blood. The extrinsic factors (on the right side) are those provided by the injured tissues. In examining the lower portion of the diagram, you can see the common pathway, which begins with the formation of prothrombin and ends with a fibrin clot. Although the pathways have begun in different ways, they each continue on the common pathway and end with the same result—clot formation.

The Start-up Process

When we are physically injured, the extrinsic pathway starts the coagulation cascade with the tissue factors. Intrinsic pathway factors then join in.

Activation of the intrinsic pathway happens in a different way. It is known that a blood clot can form within the circulatory system when a coronary thrombosis, or heart attack, occurs. In such a case the intrinsic pathway has been triggered and a clot forms. One cause of this may be a buildup of plaque along a blood vessel wall. Then, platelets begin to aggregate in this area, and the intrinsic pathway takes over, forming microscopic clots, which grow and begin to move in the circulation. So it is clear that if the conditions are right, the coagulation cascade has the ability to start up in either pathway.

Final Stages of Coagulation

A blood clot covering a wound is really a clump of platelets and blood cells trapped in fibrin. The clot prevents blood from further escaping the damaged blood vessels. Tissue cells beneath the clot start to build up the damaged tissue, and the blood clot gradually disintegrates.

Deficiencies of the Coagulation System

Blood coagulation tests are designed to judge the ability of blood to clot in a normal length of time in a test tube. When these test results show that clot formation is prolonged, the cause must be found.

A clinical laboratory scientist begins with a battery of screening tests. When one or two of these tests are abnormal, more complex testing procedures are needed. After the abnormality is found, a patient is treated with the missing or malfunctioning coagulation factor.

Treating Coagulation Disorders

Blood components is a term used to describe the products of the blood-clotting system, which are therapies used to treat coagulation disorders. The components are derived from blood that becomes available in blood banks. When they are provided, a patient can return to a normal life. The process used for obtaining these blood components is described in the blood bank chapter of this book.

SECTION 2. TESTS USED FOR DETECTING COAGULATION DISORDERS

Introduction

Tests for coagulation studies are difficult to explain and to understand. They are performed by competent clinical laboratory scientists who have had experience in this type of testing. Before discussing the coagulation tests, I would like to present a brief explanation of the theory behind this type of testing, which is performed using the patient's plasma.

First recall that plasma is blood that has an anticoagulant added so it does not clot. The straw-colored plasma is removed from the cells and used for test procedures. A comparison between plasma and serum shows that plasma contains the clotting factors and serum does not because serum is the fluid expressed when blood is allowed to clot. Therefore, the clotting factors have been used up.

Just as there were screening tests for blood cell disorders in hematology, there are screening tests for the coagulation system. The ones most often used are a platelet count, a bleeding time (BT), a prothrombin time (PT), an activated partial thromboplastin time (APTT),and a thrombin time (TT). You may be familiar with the acronyms for these tests because they appear on your clinical laboratory report when your physician requests them. The screening tests are an essential first step when a coagulation disorder is suspected. Your physician bases this suspicion on the symptoms you present and your family history.

When one of the coagulation screening tests reveals an abnormal result, the cause must be found. For example, the BT, the PT, and the APTT are usually the first ones to show that something is wrong. This has been determined by a clinical scientist because while carrying on the PT and APTT, the test tube containing a patient's plasma shows a delay when the formation of an artificial clot is timed. The test is then reported as a "prolonged" result. The formation of this clot is the end point of the test and is so important that we *time* it. It is this measurement that must be within the reference range of the test being performed.

When there is a "prolonged" clot formation, the test result is not in the desired range, which signals that further tests should be done to identify the underlying problem. More complex test procedures will help find out whether the tissue factors or the blood factors in the coagulation cascade are faulty.

The way we use a test to find the answer to a clotting problem is rather complicated, but a simple explanation is given here. If a patient bleeds for a long time when cut, one of the elements needed for clotting is missing or not functioning right. This element must be found. A test is performed with a patient's plasma as one part. A second part comprises test solutions (reagents) that provide the suspected factor the patient may be missing. In other words, the reagent could "fill in" for a deficiency of the patient's coagulation system, or it could not because at this point, we do not know what the patient's clotting problem is—the test results will tell us. We must choose the tests that will tell us the missing factor or nonfunctioning element.

An artificial, colorless fibrin clot forms within a specified time if all conditions in the test system are normal. If a factor is absent or not functioning properly, formation of the clot will be prolonged.

Certain tests detect the presence or absence of each blood-clotting element and factor in the clotting system. A clinical laboratory scientist has to find out which test combinations will provide the answer to the patient's problem.

The reference ranges for all these tests can be found in the clinical laboratory report when your physician requests them. Now for the tests themselves—there are many more than those described here, but these are the ones that are most used.

The Most Common Tests

Some tests measure whether the extrinsic pathway is functioning properly, and others measure whether the intrinsic pathway is doing its job. In each description, the pathway being tested is mentioned.

Activated Partial Thromboplastin Time

This test measures the coagulation factors of the intrinsic pathway found mainly in the blood. When we perform the APTT, if the artificial clot takes a longer-than-normal time to form, we say that the APTT is "prolonged." This means that there is a problem with a factor in the intrinsic pathway, and further tests will find which one is at fault. The reference range for the APTT is twenty-five to thirty-eight seconds.

Bleeding Time

This is a screening test used to judge the platelet and tissue factors. A small puncture wound to the pad of a finger or the ear lobe is made. Simultaneously, a stop watch is started. The bleeding is observed at measured intervals. As a drop of blood forms, it is blotted with absorbant paper. When blood can no longer be blotted, clotting has taken place. At this exact point, the watch is stopped. The number of minutes that have elapsed is the bleeding time.

We are actually measuring the time it takes the patient's coagulation system to form a clot and close a small blood vessel wound. The reference range for a bleeding time is two to eight minutes.

Coagulation Factor Assay (Analysis)

This test assesses whether a clotting factor is functioning efficiently by measuring its "percent activity." In other words, it tells us whether the factor in question is doing one-quarter, one-third, or one-half of the job it should be.

For example, a patient has bleeding symptoms, and the screening tests point to a Factor VIII deficiency. A clinical laboratory scientist must determine the actual amount of clotting activity the patient's Factor VIII generates. If it is found to be functioning at a low level, a Factor VIII blood component is provided as treatment.

The percent activity of other factors in the coagulation cascade is determined in the same way using the appropriate reagents for the factor in question.

Prothrombin Time

This test evaluates the clotting factors in the extrinsic pathway. When an artificial clot in this test takes a longer-than-normal time to form, we know that one of the factors of the extrinsic pathway is at fault. We say that the PT is "prolonged," and further tests are necessary to find out the cause. The reference range is twelve to fourteen seconds.

Thrombin Time

This test measures the efficiency of the last important step in the coagulation cascade—the conversion of fibrinogen to a biochemically stable fibrin clot. Fibrin is the main ingredient of a clot and has an important function at the wound site because it helps stop blood flow. The reference range depends upon the type of thrombin reagent used and typically is twenty to twenty-nine seconds.

SECTION 3. DISORDERS OF THE COAGULATION SYSTEM

Disseminated Intravascular Coagulation (DIC)

In this serious and rare condition, platelets and coagulation factors are used up because clotting occurs in a patient for unknown reasons. The cause must be found. The coagulation cascade has been triggered by certain biochemical compounds circulating in the blood, which uses up these two key ingredients that are necessary for normal clot formation.

DIC happens as a secondary event when a patient's entire system has been compromised. Some conditions that can cause DIC to occur include a severe infection, rare complications of pregnancy, a malignancy, and an unexpected shock to the system. Damage to blood vessels can occur in these conditions. As a result, tiny clots form within them, and it is possible for DIC to begin. At any time in the progress of disseminated intravascular coagulation, a clot may form or bleeding may occur in a patient. All the screening tests, including the PT, APTT, thrombin time, and the platelet count, reveal abnormal results.

DIC must be carefully monitored by both a clinical laboratory scientist with testing and a physician with medication. Treatment of the underlying cause of the DIC is quickly undertaken while the blood volume in a patient is maintained. The ability of the blood to clot must also be maintained so that blood factors used up by the disorder are replaced with the necessary blood components. Disseminated intravascular coagulation is a difficult treatment problem for a physician.

Factor VIII Deficiency (Hemophilia)

In this hereditary bleeding disorder, there is a deficiency in blood coagulation Factor VIII. The amount of circulating Factor VIII is not sufficient for normal blood clotting to take place. A person with this disorder may suffer bleeding into the joints and muscles or easy bruising, with the appearance of bruises on the body for seemingly unknown reasons. When these patients have surgery, there may be postoperative bleeding into the tissues where the surgery took place.

The preliminary tests for hemophilia are the APTT, which is prolonged, and the PT, which is normal. The bleeding time and platelet count are also normal. As you know from your reading, the APTT tells us whether the intrinsic pathway is working well. This combination of test results points to an intrinsic fault and a possible Factor VIII deficiency.

We then perform a test to find out the amount of activity of coagulation Factor VIII. We will find that it is deficient. Treatment is started with the blood component to provide Factor VIII.

Factor IX Deficiency

This condition is similar to Factor VIII deficiency. The outward signs are the presence of tiny, hemorrhagic spots on the skin called petechiae. There is also bleeding of mucous membranes in different areas of the body.

The screening test results are the same as in a Factor VIII

deficiency because both are present in the intrinsic pathway—the APTT is prolonged, and the PT is normal. The bleeding time and platelet count are normal. Another test is needed to distinguish between a Factor VIII and a Factor IX deficiency. A Factor IX assay must be performed to find out its activity range because although coagulation test results are similar for diagnosing these two deficiencies, the treatment is different.

Liver Disease

It is important for you to know that the liver produces most of the clotting factors. Therefore, liver disease of any kind results in a decreased production of them, compromising the clotting system. Both the PT and APTT tests are prolonged because both intrinsic and extrinsic factors are deficient or, worse still, absent. With these test results, the physician will look for possible liver disorders.

Platelet Deficiencies

A normal number of platelets is important for adequate blood clotting. But even though the actual number of platelets is normal, the way they function can be faulty, which will result in a bleeding disorder. Platelets have two important functions or properties: They adhere to things, and they aggregate, or form clusters. In case of injury to a blood vessel, platelets must adhere to the exposed surfaces of the vessel. This means that when all of the microscopic tissue layers are opened by injury, the platelets are first on the scene. They must then aggregate, forming a cluster to plug up the opening. Both of these properties are tested for in a clinical laboratory. When either one is found to be deficient, the physician prescribes treatment to augment the platelets.

Vitamin K Deficiency

This vitamin is abundant in eggs and in green, leafy vegetables. Vitamin K plays an important part in the production of some coagulation factors in the liver—Factors II, VII, IX, and X. If they are missing or deficient, normal clotting does not take place.

An additional source of vitamin K is intestinal bacteria, which produce this important vitamin for us. These are an example of beneficial bacteria.

Another essential function of vitamin K is the binding of calcium in the coagulation cascade. This interaction allows some factors to take part in coagulation. If you refer to the coagulation cascade, you can see the areas where calcium ions take part.

It is clear that a vitamin K deficiency is a serious problem, and there are other occasions when a deficiency of this important vitamin can occur, for example, a patient who has had surgery and is being fed intravenously. Fresh foods are missing from the diet, so vitamin K is low. A deficiency can also result when patients are on high doses of antibiotics. In this instance, the beneficial bacteria are being destroyed along with the pathogens, and, as a result, vitamin K production lags.

Testing for this deficiency shows that the APTT and PT are prolonged, meaning both the intrinsic and extrinsic coagulation pathways are deficient. When vitamin K therapy is provided, the coagulation test values return to normal within twenty-four hours.

Von Willebrand's Disease

In this disease, the patient experiences mild mucous membrane bleeding and nose bleeding. When women have it, there may be profuse menstrual bleeding. Easy bruising is another symptom.

Diagnostic tests are those that judge platelet function. The hallmark of this disorder is that the platelets do not function normally, even though there is a normal number of them.

The PT is normal. The APTT is prolonged, pointing to a problem of the intrinsic pathway. So far, the findings are the same as those of a Factor VIII deficiency. But in this disorder, the platelets are not doing their job so the bleeding time is also prolonged. This test result distinguishes von Willebrand's disease from a Factor VIII deficiency in which, you may remember, the bleeding time is normal.

Further tests are performed to verify that platelet adhesion and/or cluster formation are faulty. If this is so, the diagnosis is von Willebrand's disease. The patient is treated with fresh or fresh frozen plasma or cryoprecipitate (substances containing Factor VIII) to correct the deficiency.

Additional information can be obtained in Denise M. Harmening, *Clinical Hematology and Fundamentals of Hemostasis* (Philadelphia: F. A. Davis, 1997).

chapter 4

Clinical Chemistry

SECTION 1. INTRODUCTION

In the clinical chemistry laboratory, plasma, serum, and occasionally urine are tested to measure substances that keep us alive and healthy or those that should be eliminated from the blood. These biochemicals are usually part of a body system, such as the system that digests food we eat, the gastro-intestinal tract, or the organ that eliminates toxic substances, the liver. The health of our hearts is also assessed in clinical chemistry. This organ pumps blood through our arteries, bringing energy to all body parts, and our veins take away waste products. We test the products of these systems to find out whether they are within normal, healthy limits.

This may seem complicated, but as this chapter unfolds, you will develop a good understanding of your body metabolism and why clinical scientists measure its products.

What the Tests Tell Us

A serum glucose test helps a physician assess our carbohydrate metabolism. As you probably know, carbohydrates are sugars and starches. There are tests that give us information about the way our kidneys are functioning, such as the urea nitrogen (BUN) and creatinine. Serum calcium and phosphorus tests provide an insight into calcium metabolism and bone health. Testing serum for liver enzymes and for bilirubin helps us learn about liver and gallbladder health. A uric acid test tells us something about the status of cellular and nucleic acid metabolism. Enzyme tests have many uses, including the diagnosis of heart disease. Cholesterol and triglyceride tests reveal facts about our lipid (fat) metabolism. The total protein test gives us clues about kidney and liver function and physiological water balance in our bodies. Protein tests also give us information about the liver. Sodium and potassium tests help a physician find out whether a patient has an electrolyte imbalance.

In this chapter each system and its functions are described, followed by a discussion of the tests that let us know whether a system is working well. Finally, disorders that could result from these errors in metabolism are presented.

Your Physician and You

When searching for the answer to a difficult diagnostic problem, a physician can request a panel of tests that may provide the answer to chief complaints described by a patient. The physician notes these complaints, the physical symptoms he observes, and the patient's family history of disorders before devising a working diagnosis. The clinical laboratory test results and certain requested x-rays aim to prove this temporary diagnosis.

What Are Test Panels All About?

The use of automated instruments throughout the clinical laboratory has resulted in the introduction of test panels in clinical chemistry. These large "autoanalyzers" can be programmed to perform a group of tests whose results indicate whether an organ or a system is working normally. Examples include a liver function panel and a basic metabolic panel. (You can view the tests in these panels in the tables that follow.) These panels are expensive, so a physician may prefer to request individual tests applicable to the diagnosed disorder. Some insurance companies may only pay for certain tests required to make a diagnosis.

Hepatic Function Panel	Basic Metabolic Panel
albumin	carbon dioxide (bicarbonate)
bilirubin	chloride
phosphatase, alkaline	creatinine
transferase, aspartate (AST)	glucose
transferase, alanine (ALT)	potassium
	sodium
	urea nitrogen

Reference values (normal values) for test results can be found on your clinical laboratory report when you request it of your physician. The way the clinical laboratory determines the reference values for each analyte is a prolonged process.

The result is that the analyte being tested—whether it be glucose, urea, or protein—falls within the acceptable range of test values. The reference range of a substance is determined by testing a representative population in a defined state of health.

SECTION 2. BLOOD GLUCOSE

A frequently used test is the blood glucose, commonly called blood sugar, which can inform us about a serious disorder, diabetes. The test result tells us how a patient's body uses sugars and starches. Glucose is an energy-producing carbohydrate, and when the body malfunctions in its glucose usage, the disorder is called diabetes.

Sugar is found in many foods—candy and baked goods are not its only source. A variety of starches we eat are converted to sugar by enzymes in our saliva and in stomach secretions. Sugar is then absorbed into the blood plasma through tiny blood vessels in our small intestine walls. In order for body tissues to use glucose for energy, glucose must enter the tissue cells in our muscles, brain, kidneys, and any other place with activity. We can conclude that glucose reaches all tissues by means of a great transport system, the circulating blood.

What Controls the Sugar?

Insulin is a hormone produced by the pancreas that controls the availability of glucose so that our body cells can use it for energy. It helps move glucose into the cells where it is needed. Excess glucose is converted to a storage compound, glycogen, and stays in the liver cells until it can be used.

Diabetes: Too Much Sugar

There are several reasons for the development of diabetes, which is too much sugar in the blood, including not enough insulin production and the body's inability to use insulin. For either of these reasons, consumed sugar cannot enter body cells to be used. Most of it remains in the bloodstream, where it can cause many problems.

A condition in which there is a high plasma level of sugar is hyperglycemia, *hyper* meaning too much and *glycemia* meaning sugar in the blood. This glucose overload remains in the bloodstream, and the excess is excreted by the kidneys— but urine should contain no sugar. Clinical scientists find this excess sugar in the urinalysis test. This may be one of the first signs of diabetes that a physician sees.

Common Forms

Diabetes mellitus, the medical term used for diabetes, has two general types, both of which revolve around insulin:

- Insulin-dependent diabetes mellitus (IDDM) was formerly called juvenile or early onset diabetes. These individuals usually have a low production of insulin by the pancreas, resulting in an elevated blood sugar level.

- In non-insulin-dependent diabetes mellitus (NIDDM), there is nothing wrong with insulin production—insulin production may increase. The problem is that body cells are unable to use insulin. In NIDDM, the patient's symptoms are not as serious as the insulin-dependent type but tend to occur in the same direction.

An Autoimmune Complication

Some forms of diabetes are strongly associated with an autoimmune condition. When this is the case, antibodies have formed against the cells that produce insulin, which results in less being available, and the patient must be given insulin medication.

What Happens When Diabetes Is Present?

The physical effects of untreated diabetes can be devastating. After having the disease for some years, the main complications include

- damage to blood vessels, resulting in arteriosclerosis (a thickening and hardening of blood vessel walls);
- neurological symptoms, especially of the feet and hands (called peripheral neuropathy);
- damage to blood vessels of the kidneys and the retina;
- incurable bacterial infections possibly resulting in gangrene and amputation;
- disturbances of fat metabolism, when present for many years.

Telltale Symptoms

Some of the patient's chief complaints and symptoms of diabetes, especially the insulin-dependent kind, are

- an increased amount of urine output and frequency of urination (called polyuria),

- excessive thirst,
- increased appetite,
- unexplained weight loss.

To explain some of the above, it must be mentioned that glucose is a diuretic and passes through the kidneys easily, taking with it water, potassium, sodium, chloride, and other electrolytes. With the body losing liquids rapidly, fluid volume is reduced, which makes the patient thirsty. As fluids are consumed, the body fluid volume returns to normal. This cycle repeats constantly until the diabetes is discovered. It must then be controlled with proper diet and medication. In the meantime, the loss of electrolytes produces many other metabolic imbalances and causes serious problems if the condition is neglected.

In NIDDM the mentioned symptoms are present to a lesser degree. There may also be obesity and circulatory problems in this milder form of diabetes.

Hypoglycemia, Too Little Glucose in Blood

When there is a low plasma level of glucose, a condition that is the opposite of diabetes, hypoglycemia, becomes evident. Hypoglycemia can occur when the pancreas produces an excess amount of insulin. Because there is too much in the plasma, a large amount of glucose moves from the bloodstream into body cells. You may recall that insulin's job is to allow glucose to enter cells, where it is used for energy. In this disorder, there is not enough glucose in the blood to carry on all the body functions.

Glucagon: The Counterbalance

Another cause of hypoglycemia that is not as common is a hormone imbalance. Glucagon is a balancing hormone that opposes the action of insulin. If there is not enough glucagon, insulin has a free range of action. Some of the symptoms of hypoglycemia are faintness, weakness, sweating, a rapid heartbeat, hunger, and nervousness.

Hypoglycemia is detected when the reference value for a fasting glucose test is below fifty milligrams in each deciliter of serum or plasma. The lower test limit of a normal fasting serum glucose is seventy milligrams, so you can see that the hypoglycemic person has a test value well below that.

Glucose Testing—Plasma or Serum Glucose Test

This test uses a biochemical enzyme reaction to determine the amount of glucose present in a sample. The reference range for a fasting serum or plasma glucose is found on the clinical laboratory report when requested by your physician. The current acceptable fasting blood glucose level according to the American Diabetes Association is less than or equal to 126 milligrams in each deciliter of serum. The diagnosis of diabetes is made when the test results are greater than or equal to 126 milligrams on at least two occasions.

Quality Control of a Serum Glucose Specimen

The specimen for glucose determination is plasma or serum from a blood sample usually taken from a vein in the arm. It is collected in a vacuum-fitted test tube with an anticoagulant present to prevent the blood from clotting.

When the test is delayed for a few hours, an undesirable biochemical action takes place called glycolysis, which means literally a dissolving of sugar. During glycolysis white blood cells, red blood cells, platelets, and bacteria (when present) in the tube of blood destroy some of the sugar. The result is a glucose value that is lower than the actual one. Therefore, in an accredited clinical laboratory, when testing is going to be delayed for more than an hour, the plasma is removed from the cellular elements and stored in a refrigerator until tested.

The Oral Glucose Tolerance Test (OGTT)— An Early Aid to Final Diagnosis

When a physician receives the result of a fasting glucose test outside of the reference range, the next step is an oral glucose tolerance test (OGTT), which is also used to discover hidden or latent diabetes. The test requires the cooperation of a nurse, a clinical laboratory scientist, and the patient and challenges a patient's biochemical pathway for glucose metabolism.

There are several types of glucose tolerance tests. A preliminary one used after discovering an abnormal fasting blood sugar is the two-hour oral glucose tolerance test. Others are the three-hour and four-hour OGTT. The extra time is an attempt to study the problem in a patient more closely to arrive at a definitive diagnosis.

Physicians have a choice as to which test they will use for a diagnosis. Some use only one procedure, while others use several. For example, if the two-hour oral glucose tolerance test does not clearly define the problem, then a longer version of a glucose tolerance test is used.

The Test Procedure

An oral dose of glucose in the form of a drink is given to the patient. Then, a blood sample is drawn at hourly intervals. The test results of one or more samples must be two hundred or more milligrams of glucose per deciliter of serum for a diagnosis of diabetes.

Glucose Monitoring at Home

It is possible for a diabetic person to test his or her blood in the comfort of home. A drop of capillary blood obtained from the finger with a lancet or needle is added to a reagent strip. The resulting color is matched on a color chart to estimate roughly the amount of glucose present.

Another option is the use of a small glucose monitoring instrument available to diabetics for testing at home. Current advances make it possible to use an instrument that combines a lancet and an automatic measuring device to test for glucose. Several models need only a few drops of blood for the test.

Glycosylated Hemoglobin (Glycohemoglobin) Test

This method for measuring sugar in the blood uses a whole blood specimen and determines the amount of a certain form of hemoglobin referred to as A_{1c}, or glycosylated hemoglobin. It is formed by the binding of glucose and hemoglobin during the life span of a red blood cell, which is normally 120 days. Therefore, the test provides physicians with a measure of the effectiveness of their treatment of diabetes over a period of three to four months.

The reference range for glycohemoglobin is 3 percent to 6

percent in nondiabetics and from 12 percent to 21 percent in diabetics. A distinct advantage of this method is that the physician is able to discover whether the patient is following a diabetic diet between visits and taking prescribed medicines.

Still Another Way to Find Excess Sugar

I have mentioned that glucose is present in a urine sample when a person has diabetes. The urinalysis clinical laboratory routinely tests urine for sugar, which is useful in detecting one of the first signs of diabetes. Normally, none should be present. Sugar's presence alerts the physician to investigate further.

When sugar is excreted by the kidneys, the condition is called glucosuria, an important early sign of the possibility of diabetes. However, the test estimates sugar in the urine. If the patient's kidneys have a high threshold for sugar, the test may be negative. In other words, the blood sugar is high, but the kidneys can tolerate this level, and sugar will not be excreted. Then, the physician must rely on chief complaints, signs, symptoms, and finally blood sugar studies.

SECTION 3. THE RENAL SYSTEM—OUR VITAL KIDNEYS

Urea and Creatinine

The kidneys are important organs that contribute to our good health. We have two of them, one located on either side of the spinal column above the waist. Microscopic blood vessels in each kidney filter our blood to get rid of waste products, which are passed in our urine. You could say that as blood circulates through them, it is cleansed by our kidneys.

The renal system consists of the kidneys, ureters, bladder, and urethra. The two ureters connect each kidney with the urinary bladder. The urethra delivers urine from the bladder to the outside. There are several products of this filtration process, and testing for them gives us a good idea of how the kidneys are working. Urea is one of these products; creatinine is another. We will discuss both of these organic waste products. A drawing of the urinary system follows.

Urea Production

Urea, often referred to as blood urea nitrogen (BUN), is a by-product of the breakdown of amino acids, which occurs in the liver. In the beginning, amino acids enter our bodies in the protein foods we eat. They provide fuel for energy production. If our diets are high in protein, urea production is greater. This waste product of body chemistry must be eliminated by the kidneys.

Creatinine: A Significant Waste Product

Testing for the presence of creatinine is another way to assess kidney function. Creatinine is a waste product of body chemistry, but more importantly, it is a by-product of muscle activity. So it follows that plasma creatinine levels depend on our body muscle mass. The greater the amount of muscle a person has, the higher the normal creatinine level. The normal range of test values for creatinine allows for this difference between small and large muscle mass in an individual.

Another important fact to notice when observing creatinine is that its test value reflects kidney function better than

The urinary tract

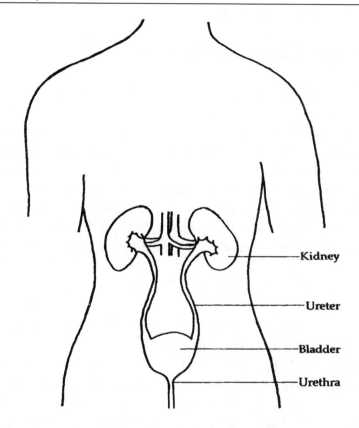

Kidney

Ureter

Bladder

Urethra

urea's test value does. The reason is that urea production is altered by our food intake and the digestive process. Therefore, to judge kidney function, a physician may request both a plasma creatinine and a urea nitrogen test.

An exception to using these tests as an indicator of kidney malfunction is the following situation. If a patient has bleeding in the stomach or intestinal region, the BUN becomes elevated. This bleeding must be discovered by a physician who may suspect kidney problems because of the high BUN test result.

Important Functions of Kidneys

As previously mentioned, the main function of kidneys is to filter blood to eliminate waste products. Important products of body metabolism, such as water, minerals, and reusable biochemicals, are saved by the kidneys. These substances recirculate in the bloodstream because they can be used again.

Another function of the kidneys is to maintain water content in the body by regulating urinary output. When the right amount of water is maintained, electrolytes are kept in balance. You will find out more about electrolytes later in this chapter.

Warning Signs of a Failing Kidney

When urea and creatinine values are well above the reference ranges, the body is keeping waste products instead of eliminating them. It is a startling fact that approximately 50 percent of normal kidney function is lost before the urea and creatinine values rise above the reference ranges. In order to stop this from happening, a physician depends upon a good preliminary test for kidney function, the urinalysis, an important test requested routinely when a patient is seen for the first time. When kidney disease is suspected, this test is of vital importance.

Diseases of the Renal System

Chronic Kidney Failure

Chronic kidney failure is progressive loss of kidney function. There are a variety of reasons for this, some of them obvious and others obscure. There may be a birth defect of the renal system, causing a disorder early in life. Other causes are the presence of bacterial infections, or the patient may be experiencing a toxic effect of drugs being taken for other illnesses.

Additional causes for kidney problems in mature people are a diminished blood flow through the kidney because of lack of exercise, a low fluid intake, and, most importantly, vascular diseases such as atherosclerosis and diabetes. A tumor or a calculus (sometimes called a stone) may actually be blocking the path of urine somewhere in the excretory system. These can all result in chronic kidney failure.

When the kidneys fail to function from time to time, there is a mild accumulation of waste products in the blood. If it is not detected and treated, a more severe kidney condition may develop. The signs of this show up in a urinalysis test with the finding of protein in the urine. The medical term for this is proteinuria. Because the waste products building up in the blood include urea nitrogen and creatinine, these test values increase in the serum. When blood cells and pus appear in the urine as a result of this condition, the urine protein values are positive.

Acute Renal Failure

In the acute later stages of renal failure, an anemia and an imbalance of body electrolytes develop. An accumulation of waste products (especially urea) in the blood is called azotemia. If not treated promptly, it is followed by uremia, a toxic condition brought on by an overwhelming amount of waste products in the system.

A patient with uremia suffers from weakness, fatigue, loss of appetite, and decline of muscle strength. It is a serious condition and must be monitored by a physician with the aid of regular clinical laboratory testing.

Relief from Some of the Problems

Patients with acute and chronic renal disease make use of hemodialysis, also referred to as kidney dialysis. The procedure uses an artificial kidney and the patient's blood. Between periods when hemodialysis is used, uremia develops as the kidney begins to fail again. Then dialysis is repeated. An explanation of hemodialysis is found in the glossary.

A permanent solution for patients with this condition is a kidney transplant.

Tests for Kidney Function

- Urea nitrogen. This assesses kidney function and is sometimes referred to as a blood urea nitrogen determination. An elevated urea value means that the body is retaining waste products instead of eliminating them in urine. Therefore, a high plasma urea concentration usually indicates impaired kidney function. The reference range for urea nitrogen is eight to twenty-six milligrams in each deciliter of serum.

- Calcium and phosphorus determinations are performed regularly.

- Creatinine. If the value for creatinine is elevated, the physician requests additional clinical tests for assessing kidney function. The reference range for creatinine is 0.5 to 1.2 milligrams in each deciliter of plasma or serum.

- Electrolyte determinations. The sodium and potassium levels are monitored with regular testing.

- Urinalysis. This is a relatively inexpensive test requested routinely by physicians and is a valuable source of information about how kidneys are functioning. Testing for the presence of the protein albumin is an important part of urinalysis. In the normal kidney, only a small amount of protein is filtered at the glomerulus and is passed on with the urine. The presence of measurable quantities is a sign of temporary or chronic kidney failure.

SECTION 4. CALCIUM AND PHOSPHORUS

Their Importance in Our Diets

We have been made aware from many sources of the importance of calcium in our meals. We find it in cheese, milk, yogurt, cottage cheese, ice cream, and some vegetables. It is necessary to replenish this mineral every day because calcium in our system combines with phosphates to form bone. If the calcium test value is outside of the normal range, a request for a serum phosphorus test is usually made. We need both substances to have strong bones.

Although it seems to be a passive organ, bone is really a dynamic one, physiologically active throughout our lifetime.

The Metabolic Path of Calcium

After we eat and digest milk and other dairy products, calcium is present in the bloodstream. During the digestive process, calcium, in order to be absorbed, requires phosphorus and vitamin D. Most foods we eat contain an abundance of phosphorus, so we need not worry about getting enough of that. However, our diets must have sufficient calcium to combine with the phosphorus to make the building blocks for bone.

What Does Calcium Do for Us?

There are many important functions of calcium, including the formation, maintenance, and repair of the bones in our bodies. Calcium also takes part in muscle contraction by maintaining the right degree of neuromuscular excitability and tone. If you have read the chapter on coagulation, you know that calcium acts on enzymes that control blood clotting. You can see this graphically when you refer to the coagulation cascade diagram. It is clear that the level of calcium in plasma is important for normal body functioning, but what controls the blood level of this important element?

Control of Calcium and Phosphorus Levels

The answer lies in two tiny glands embedded in thyroid tissue known as the parathyroid glands, which secrete parathyroid hormone (PTH). This hormone raises the plasma level of calcium by acting on cells that contain calcium, located in bone. PTH causes these cells to release the calcium and phosphorus into surrounding tissue and eventually into the bloodstream. All this activity takes place when more calcium is needed by the body, for example, when bone is being repaired in another location or calcium is being lost somewhere in the body and the calcium from bone will be used to replace it.

Systems Need to Be in Good Working Order

You can understand that in order to get the most out of the food we eat, all body systems must be functioning well in delivering nutrients where they are needed. As for calcium in our blood, the right level depends upon a normal secretion pattern of the parathyroid gland. A second important factor is having enough phosphates and vitamin D in our diets. We produce this vitamin by exposure to ultraviolet rays of the sun. But even when we have all of the preceding conditions met, we still need good intestinal absorption of calcium from the food we eat.

There is a greater demand on this metabolic system during childhood and adolescence, when growth occurs rapidly and bone is developing. It is important that children drink milk, which has all these nutrients in it. Another interesting fact about calcium is that when a mother nurses an infant, more calcium is absorbed from her diet because more is needed for the production of milk.

Disorders of Calcium/Phosphorus Metabolism

- Rickets. This is a disorder that results from a calcium deficiency. It occurs in infants and young children and is characterized by softening of bones. It is usually accompanied by skeletal deformities in the legs because they bear the body's weight. Vitamin D deficiency may also cause this problem because the vitamin is needed for the body to use calcium. Milk that we purchase from the store has vitamin D added to it. Scoliosis, a lateral curvature of the spine, can also result from this disorder.

- Malabsorption. This springs from a variety of causes, some of which are discussed in the hematology chapter because they may cause an anemia. We know that calcium needs vitamin D to be absorbed. Vitamin D needs fat or lipids to be absorbed. Even though calcium is consumed, it is not entering the bloodstream because of the fat malabsorption problem. The result is low blood calcium levels, even though the mineral is present in the diet.

- Hyperparathyroidism. This is a long word for a disorder in which there is increased activity of the parathyroid glands with more secretion of the hormone. Tumors developing in the tissue of these glands have the same effect. Both conditions result in more parathyroid hormone being released into the blood and an increase of calcium levels. You may recall that PTH acts on bone cells, causing them to release calcium. Hyperparathyroidism results in diminished bone strength.

- Metastatic carcinoma of bone. When carcinoma invades and breaks down bone tissue, calcium is released into the blood. Carcinoma refers to a malignant neoplasm that can invade other tissue. If the invasion of bone is massive, the calcium level rises. When there is only slight destruction of bone, the kidneys can excrete the excess calcium.

Testing

Indications

When faulty calcium metabolism is suspected, testing for calcium and phosphorus levels will verify this. Tests that determine whether the parathyroid glands are functioning normally assist a physician in identifying and managing bone disease. Some tests reveal parathyroid dysfunction, but the tests for serum calcium and phosphorus levels are a good start.

Specimen and Reference Ranges for Calcium and Phosphorus

The type of specimen for calcium determination is serum or plasma collected from a patient who has had nothing to eat or drink for ten to twelve hours.

The adult reference range for calcium is 8.8 to 10.5 milligrams for each deciliter of serum. The reference range for phosphorus is 2.7 to 4.5 milligrams in each deciliter of serum.

Section 5. The Liver and Gallbladder

Essential for maintaining normal body functions, the liver is the largest and most important organ of the body. Many biochemical substances our bodies use every day are produced by it. A second function, which seems to oppose the first, is the breakdown of complex biochemical compounds into simpler ones, usually resulting in energy production. For example, stored glycogen inside liver cells breaks down into glucose, which the body uses as an energy source.

The liver also rids the body of toxic substances that would be harmful if they remained in the bloodstream.

A Truly Strategic Organ

Practically all of the nutrients derived from the foods we eat that are absorbed in the intestinal tract pass through and are modified by the liver. Liver cells use these nutrients to build essential substances, which circulate in the blood and are used by different body tissues. Some of these compounds are described in the following paragraphs.

The Liver and Fat

Fats in the food we eat are biochemically broken down by liver cells for energy. If there is more fat than we need for the tasks at hand, the excess is converted into fatty tissue. It is preserved there in long-term storage to be used when we need extra energy.

The Liver and Proteins

Most body proteins are produced in liver tissue and then used for different body functions. Some examples are the proteins we need for blood clotting and albumin, which helps maintain body water balance. Apoproteins carry hormones all over the body wherever they are needed, and immunoglobulin proteins are needed to maintain our immunity.

The Liver and Bilirubin

A pigment called bilirubin is formed and excreted by the liver. Bilirubin comes from old and weakened red blood cells. When the spleen destroys them because they can no longer do their job, hemoglobin is released. You may recall that hemoglobin is the main substance inside red blood cells. The spleen breaks down the hemoglobin and releases bilirubin, iron, and the protein globin.

In the bloodstream, bilirubin combines with the carrier albumin, which transports it to the liver. Inside liver cells, enzymes convert bilirubin into a form that allows it to move in and out of liver cells. It moves in the tiny canals of the liver with bile until it reaches the gallbladder. Bile is stored in the gallbladder and is released into the small intestine to help digest fats.

The Fate of Bile

When bile is needed in the small intestine, many biochemical reactions take place, and their product is a family of compounds known as the urobilinogens. A fraction of these compounds is excreted in urine and feces as urobilin and stercobilin. These darkly colored compounds give urine a straw-yellow color and feces a brown color.

A sign of liver problems is a change in the color of urine. A light-colored stool and dark-colored urine (the opposite of normal) indicate that there may be a blockage of the bile ducts by calculi (stones) or a tumor. Further tests are used to find the cause of this blockage, which could be located in the gall-bladder, the liver, or the pancreas.

Testing for Liver Disease

Several clinical laboratory tests provide a physician with information about liver function. Some of them are mentioned here.

- Bilirubin determination provides information about the liver and gallbladder. An increase in bilirubin may mean there is a hemolytic process going on. That is, more red blood cells are being destroyed than is normal; therefore, excess bilirubin is released. You may recall that old or defective red blood cells are eliminated by the spleen. The physician must investigate this increase with tests for anemia.
- Urinalysis detects increased amounts of bilirubin and urobilinogen in urine.
- A total protein test measures the amount of the proteins albumin and globulin in the bloodstream. (Proteins are discussed later in this chapter.)
- Prothrombin time, a coagulation test, helps find out whether the liver is producing enough coagulation proteins.
- Liver enzyme determinations, or testing for certain enzymes present in the liver, can tell us whether the liver is in trouble. When there is liver damage, as in hepatitis (a viral infection) or physical injury from an accident, the enzyme studies will reveal it. Enzymes are discussed later in this chapter.

Reference ranges for these tests are found in the clinical laboratory report when they are requested by your physician.

A majority of these tests are included in the "hepatic function panel" of a clinical chemistry autoanalyzer.

Diseases

Disorders Causing Abnormal Bilirubin Values

An increase in the amount of bilirubin in the serum can be due to a variety of causes. It must be investigated with further testing to find out more about liver health. Some causes are listed here.

- Red blood cells are destroyed in some anemias. Hemoglobin is released by the cells and degrades into bilirubin and related products. An increase in these products suggests that a hemolytic anemia may be present.
- When liver cells do not function normally to break down and get rid of toxic substances, bilirubin also remains in the liver. This results in high test values.
- When injury to the liver occurs as a result of viral hepatitis, alcoholic hepatitis, or cirrhosis, there will be an increase in serum bilirubin.
- Obstruction of bile ducts by gallstones and tumors results in increased serum bilirubin levels. As mentioned previously, a signal of this is a light-colored stool and dark-colored urine.

The reference range for the measurement of total bilirubin is 0.2 to 1.2 milligrams in each deciliter of serum.

The Jaundiced Patient

A high bilirubin test value can cause a condition known as jaundice. It results in a yellow coloration of the skin and whites of the eyes. A physician considers jaundice to be a sign of illness in the area of the liver and gallbladder. Therefore, the cause of jaundice is promptly investigated by testing for liver enzymes, a serum bilirubin test to learn the amount of increase, and x-ray studies.

SECTION 6. PURINES AND URIC ACID

What Happens to Proteins We Eat?

Biochemical compounds called purines—found in meat, fish, beans, and other high-protein foods we eat—are used by the body to form nucleic acids. You are familiar with deoxyribonucleic acid (DNA) and ribonucleic acid (RNA), both of which are essential in protein production. When the foods we eat are high in these nucleic acids, purines increase in our serum.

Another source of nucleic acid is inside our bodies when tissues are broken down by a long-standing infection or a malignancy. When an excess of these products accumulates in the blood, the kidneys take over and excrete them.

What Happens to Purines?

When we eat foods containing purines, several metabolic pathways can be followed, including:

1. They are changed to nucleic acid to build new cells and tissues, including blood cells.
2. They are changed to uric acid and urates, which are then excreted in urine or feces.

When our diets are high in nucleic acid–rich foods, we may have increased serum uric acid values, which are sure to rise if the kidneys do not excrete waste products as efficiently as they should.

A Disorder of High Uric Acid Levels—Gout

A common result of high uric acid levels in blood is the butt of some jokes, namely, the disease commonly known as *gout*. When food and beverages high in nucleic acid potential are consumed in excess by people with a predisposition for this disease, uric acid begins to crystalize in the tissues. As a result, microscopic sharp-edged crystals form in our joints. The target location is often the hands and feet, where less blood circulates. The sluggish flow and possibly cooler temperatures in these areas of the body promote uric acid crystal formation.

These crystals can also form when we are injured in an accident or undergo surgery. With this added physical stress, uric acid crystal formation is enhanced.

A person who suffers from gout can have sharp pain in the large toe, knee joint, knee cap, or tendons. If not treated, attacks of gout can lead to tophi formation and permanent joint deformity. Tophi are chalky deposits of sodium urate that can form in the joints and soft tissues when a person has high uric acid levels.

Clinical Testing for Uric Acid

The reference range for uric acid in serum or plasma is 4 to 8.5 milligrams in each deciliter for men and 2.7 to 7.3 for women. A physician requests it when gout is suspected in a patient.

SECTION 7. ENZYMES

An Important Undercurrent of All Body Functions

Enzymes act everywhere in the body where important jobs must be done efficiently. Clinical testing for enzymes is vital because they are present inside all body cells and are essential for normal cell function.

Active during the whole life of a cell, an enzyme is a protein whose biochemical structure speeds up chemical reactions in the body. Individual enzymes are further distinguished by favoring certain types of cells, for example, lactate dehydrogenase (LD) in heart and skeletal muscle, aspartate aminotransferase (AST) in the liver, and acid phosphatase (ACP) in prostate tissue. These acronyms can be found on your clinical laboratory report.

Enzymes are measured by the amount of activity they display in a test system. In fact, we report them in activity units, which represent the quantity of an enzyme that will speed up a reaction in a test system at a certain temperature.

All in the Enzyme Family

Most important enzymes are common to all of our cells, which makes it difficult to find the organ that is malfunctioning. We solved this problem by finding that some enzymes are present at unusually high levels in some tissues and not in others. Several important ones and causes for their increase in plasma are discussed.

Different Forms of the Same Enzyme

A physician depends on a clinical scientist to determine the level of each type of enzyme in a patient's serum. To complicate matters, each enzyme has different forms, known as isoenzymes. For example, the same enzyme can exist in liver and in heart muscle, but each one has a different biochemical structure. So it is important to identify the specific isoenzyme that is present in increased amounts in a patient.

The Case of Enzyme Balancing

Although most enzymes are present inside body cells at a higher concentration than in blood plasma, they are measured in blood, which is where enzymes flow when various cells of the body are damaged. We determine the amount of enzyme in blood plasma by comparing how much should be there with how much is actually present. In this way, when reading the test report, a physician has a good idea of the damage done to an organ. The effectiveness of treatment is tracked with daily tests through the course of the illness.

Stages of Enzymes

The estimated level that is "normal" for an enzyme in plasma is really a balance between three stages in its life cycle. One is the formation of it in a cell, then the release of it into plasma during the life of a cell, and finally the rate of clearance of the enzyme from the bloodstream.

For diagnostic purposes, the plasma level is the most important stage, especially when we have a disease to investigate. You recall that this is when damaged cells release more enzyme into the blood. So damage is evident in our test results.

An Increase—But Why?

There are several ways these variations of enzyme levels in plasma can occur.

- The rate of cell destruction may increase, releasing more of the enzyme into plasma. An example is hepatitis, in which liver cells die and release such enzymes as AST and ALT.
- If tumors are growing in an organ, the increased cell activity causes more enzymes to be released.
- When an organ has been injured in an accident, additional enzymes are released.

Small changes in concentration of one or two of these enzymes can be detected. These tests can lead to early detection of tumors or localized tissue damage to an organ.

Close Tracking Pays Off

After obtaining a high enzyme concentration from a patient, a physician keeps track of the level of enzyme activity from day to day by regular testing. For example, there may be drastic damage to liver cells in response to a viral hepatitis infection. Very high plasma levels of liver aspartate aminotransferase (AST) are present on the first day. This level gradually falls as the enzyme is cleared from the plasma and as the damaged liver cells are repaired. For this reason, daily enzyme testing during a serious illness is valuable. Another advantage is the doctor finds out whether treatment is helping.

By this time, you probably want to know something about individual enzymes. In the next few pages, some families of enzymes are named and something about each is mentioned. Then, disorders that affect enzyme concentration are noted.

Enzyme I. Aminotransferases

The Importance of the Aminotransferases

There are two aminotransferase enzymes, which are widely distributed in the body.

- High concentrations of aspartate aminotransferase (AST) are present in the heart, liver, skeletal muscle, kidneys, and red blood cells.
- High concentrations of alanine aminotransferase (ALT) are present in the liver, with a smaller amount in skeletal muscle, the kidneys, and the heart.

Disorders of AST and ALT

Aspartate aminotransferase. The plasma levels of AST are high in coronary thrombosis (heart attack), viral hepatitis, and liver necrosis. If a liver problem can be eliminated by the physician, a high level may be because of a heart condition, and further tests must investigate heart health.

High AST values are also obtained in blood circulatory failure, leading to shock.

Moderately high levels are found in skeletal muscle disease and such traumatic conditions as cardiac surgery or severe hemolytic anemia.

Alanine aminotransferase. The levels of ALT are high in toxic hepatitis, viral hepatitis, and blood circulatory failure. When the physician looks for a liver disorder and finds none, the possibility of blood circulatory failure arises.

Enzyme II. Lactate Dehydrogenase (LD)

Lactate dehydrogenase is present in many body tissues, but there is a high concentration in heart muscle, skeletal muscle, the liver, the kidneys, the brain, and red blood cells. Five isoenzymes of LD are detectable by the electrophoresis test and are of clinical significance when there is an increase in one of the isoenzymes from a particular organ.

LD 1 isoenzyme is present in heart muscle and the kidneys. At the other end of the spectrum, LD 5 isoenzyme is present in the liver and in skeletal muscle. LD forms 1 through 5 move at different rates in the electrophoretic cell, so we can measure them by their movement patterns.

In some illnesses, all five enzymes are increased by varying amounts. When several repeated tests show a persistent and sharp increase in one of the isoenzymes, this organ is in trouble.

Testing for LD

Because LD is present in most body tissues, including blood cells, measurement of the *total LD activity* is not very useful to a physician. The quantity of the five LD isoenzymes is much more helpful. LD reference values can be found in a clinical laboratory test report for the method used by the testing laboratory of your physician.

Some Causes of High Levels

The highest lactate dehydrogenase 1 and 2 levels are seen in patients with myocardial infarction (tissue death of heart muscle) after a heart attack and in some blood disorders. LD2 and LD3 show increases when there is extensive invasion of tissues by carcinoma and in leukemia and in circulatory failure with shock.

A physician tracks the values by requesting the test daily or as often as needed while the patient recovers.

Enzyme III. The Phosphatases

There are two phosphatase enzymes. One is active in the body where tissues are in an alkaline, or basic, environment. The other is active where conditions are more acidic.

Alkaline Phosphatase (ALP)

The alkaline phosphatases are a group of enzymes that act on organic phosphate compounds in the body in an alkaline environment. Different ones are present in a number of organs, including the liver, the kidneys, the intestinal wall, and bone in varying amounts in both adults and children. ALP in the plasma of adults is mainly from bone and the liver. The activity of several ALP isoenzymes is measured routinely in some clinical chemistry test panels.

Increases due to Normal Causes

Because the phosphates are present in so many organs, their increased activity may at some times be due to normal physiological processes. The ALP isoenzyme found in bone is important for normal bone formation. In children, where bones are actively growing, this isoenzyme is increased in the plasma. Adolescents have an increased amount during puberty, when rapid growth occurs. In adults most of the normal plasma levels of ALP are from the liver isoenzyme.

Increases due to Disorders of Bone

Metastatic carcinoma. Increases in ALP in adults are seen when cancer cells invade bone from organs and tissues where the cancer started.

Rickets. ALP is also increased in rickets, a disease in which there is not enough calcium in the diet for normal bone growth. The body chemistry removes it from bone so that calcium can be increased in the blood where it is needed. Rickets occurs in children and adults who have not had nutritionally balanced diets. The lack of calcium can result in a malformation of bones that bear weight, such as the legs and hips.

Increases due to Disorders of the Liver and Surrounding Organs

- inflammation of the gallbladder (cholecystitis) with gallstones
- tumors in the region of the liver and gallbladder
- carcinoma of the pancreas
- viral hepatitis

Acid Phosphatase (ACP)

This enzyme acts on organic phosphate compounds in the body when the surrounding environment is acidic. The acid phosphatase enzyme is found in the prostate, the liver, red blood cells, platelets, and bone.

Abnormal Values for ACP

The main use for this test has been to detect early cancer of the prostate gland. When a patient has this condition, the enzyme is markedly increased. However, the enzyme is also increased in hyperplasia, or excess cellular activity of the gland.

A Current Test for Prostate Health—The PSA Test

The prostate specific antigen test is currently used for the detection of prostate cancer. The antigen we test for is produced only by the prostate gland. Small amounts of free PSA are normally found in the bloodstream, but, in certain conditions of the prostate, the amount increases. Plasma levels of the antigen increase when there is inflammation of the prostate by benign or malignant tumor formation. PSA test levels are useful in monitoring the progress of a tumor and the patient's reaction to treatment in a patient with prostate cancer.

In making a diagnosis, a physician must consider that, as men age, the prostate enlarges and PSA levels increase. Before a diagnosis of cancer can be made, a sample of prostate tissue is obtained and examined histologically by a pathologist.

Enzyme IV. Creatine Kinase (CK)

This enzyme has three isoenzyme forms present in varying amounts in brain tissue, cardiac muscle, skeletal muscle, and the prostate. Brain tissue has a high concentration of CK, and there is a substantial amount in skeletal muscle and heart muscle.

Abnormal Values for CK—Coronary Thrombosis

Increased amounts of CK are evident in heart disease, particularly when a patient is experiencing a myocardial infarction (MI). Commonly known as a heart attack, MI refers to a necrotic area of heart muscle that has been deprived of oxygen. This damage occurs when a blood vessel that supplies nourishment to heart muscle is blocked. The blockage is referred to as a coronary thrombosis.

After a heart attack, the serum level of the heart muscle isoenzyme rises sharply within two to six hours—three to six times the normal value.

Thirty-six hours after a myocardial infarction, this level falls, but another enzyme is increased. This important indicator, sometimes called a "marker," is cardiac troponin, and its value is monitored by regular testing to follow the patient's recovery.

Cardiac Troponin: A Heart Muscle Signal

An increase in troponin provides a signal that heart muscle has been damaged. A high value of this test is found within a few hours after symptoms begin and remains elevated for up to ten days after the onset of chest pain. The test is most useful for a diagnosis in patients who are in the hospital with uncharacteristic symptoms of a heart attack. Both troponin T and troponin I forms are more specific for heart injury than creatine kinase. So it is useful when patients have vague heart attack symptoms and a normal value for the CK heart muscle isoenzyme. The troponins provide valuable information about heart damage and the future risk for a patient.

C-Reactive Protein

A substance that is thought to predict a predisposition for a cardiovascular incident is C-reactive protein. High test values have been regarded as a signal of inflammatory conditions in the body. The test is also used in the diagnosis of rheumatoid arthritis, another inflammatory disorder.

Risk Factors

It is more likely for a cardiovascular event to occur when certain risk factors are present in a person, such as hypertension, diabetes mellitus, low HDL cholesterol, current cigarette smoking, and a family history of premature coronary heart disease.

Additional Causes for Increased CK Values

- Stroke—Increases in CK brain isoenzyme values occur during cerebrovascular episodes such as strokes.
- Shock—When a patient is involved in an accident or other type of injury.
- Progressive muscular dystrophy—The most striking increases in CK muscle isoenzyme occur in the early stages of this disease.

Exclusion of Heart Disease

When these high enzyme values are obtained, a diagnosis of heart attack may be eliminated in the following conditions:

- when the patient has muscle strain causing pain, or left shoulder bursitis, or
- disorders of the esophagus, which may cause mild chest and upper back pain.

The physician's physical findings and further clinical laboratory studies aid in an accurate diagnosis.

SECTION 8. LIPIDS—THE FEAR OF THE '90S

Body Fats and Their Transport

Plasma lipids, which we commonly call "fats," are increased in concentration in various disorders, including heart disease, blood circulatory problems, and certain types of diabetes.

What We Need to Know about Fat Metabolism

You have most likely heard of the names of these lipids recently and discussed them with neighbors and friends. Some of the fat compounds we have to be cautious about are fatty acids, triglycerides, and cholesterol. Most of us are familiar with these terms because of warnings by our physician that high levels in the blood can cause illness.

How It All Starts

It may help your understanding of this complex system to follow the course of fats that we eat. After digesting them, a mixture of fats from our diets are carried in the bloodstream by chylomicrons on their way to cells in the body. Chylomicrons and very low density lipoproteins (VLDL) are very large complexes compared to other fat molecules traveling in blood. They contain mostly triglyceride and some cholesterol. If a sample of blood is taken one to two hours after a meal, the milky look of the plasma in a test tube shows that they are present. You could call them the delivery system for digested fats.

In the liver, cholesterol and triglycerides are stored, and, when necessary, they are used to form other types of fat to be used for energy.

So it is clear that after digestion, lipids circulate in the blood. This transport occurs in combination with protein, and the combination is called a lipoprotein. Different lipids are combined in various ways to form these lipoproteins. This phenomenon will become clear as you read on.

Different Forms of Fat in Blood

I will describe each type of fat in the blood.

Fatty acids (FA) are simple compounds that come from foods we eat. An immediate source of energy, they combine with glycerides and eventually form triglycerides. If not used for energy, they are stored in fat tissue.

Triglyceride is a large fat molecule made up of fatty acids in combination with glycerides.

Cholesterol is in foods we eat. In addition to this source, our liver cells are capable of producing it. Cholesterol is used in our body metabolism in many ways. Even though it is considered a "bad fat," a moderate amount is important for normal body functions.

Phospholipids are very important lipid compounds. They resemble triglycerides in structure, but each molecule contains both phosphates and a nitrogen compound, which make phospholipids soluble in water-based body fluids. This is an important quality for transport because lipids must move easily between the water-based blood plasma and tissues when they are needed for energy.

Triglycerides and cholesterol are combined in different proportions with these phospholipid molecules as a unit. Because of this combination they can travel easily between plasma and tissues as necessary.

What We Call Them

The combinations described are carried in the body as water-soluble protein complexes called lipoproteins.

From media health programs and other sources, you

have become familiar with the acronyms VLDL, LDL, and HDL, and you also know that they refer to fats. If we translate these acronyms, they become very low density lipoproteins, low density lipoproteins, and high density lipoproteins, respectively.

Each one differs in size and composition. For example, all have different amounts of protein carrier for traveling purposes. The higher the content of protein carrier, the less chance of atherosclerosis (hardening of the arteries) occurring.

Dissecting the Lipoproteins

In order to understand these lipid structures, we will break them down into their individual components.

- HDL is composed mainly of the protein carrier and phospholipid, with some cholesterol.
- LDL mainly comprises cholesterol, with substantial amounts of protein carrier and phospholipid.
- VLDL is mostly triglyceride, with lesser amounts of cholesterol and phospholipid.
- Chylomicrons are composed mostly of triglycerides, with small amounts of cholesterol and phospholipid.

Caution Signs

Cholesterol in the lipoprotein molecule is commonly talked about in terms of *good* and *bad*. You may be interested in what these terms mean when applied to the body lipids we have discussed.

- Good cholesterol is the high density lipoproteins (HDL). They are responsible for removing cholesterol from artery walls and taking it to the liver, where it is broken down and eliminated. When high levels of HDL are present, there is less chance of heart disease.
- Bad cholesterol is low density lipoproteins (LDL), also referred to as LDL cholesterol, which helps to deposit fat onto artery walls. Excess LDL cholesterol leads to atherosclerosis.
- Bad cholesterol is also very low density lipoproteins (VLDL), which transport triglycerides. Increased triglycerides are associated with greater risk of coronary heart disease.

At this point, you begin to understand why your physician tries to keep your HDL high and your VLDL and LDL at low levels.

The Beneficial Side of Lipids

The presence of these lipids in blood provides us with fat to burn for energy or fat to store for later use. Because chylomicrons and VLDL have high triglyceride content, low levels in the bloodstream are desirable. LDL and HDL have a substantial amount of protein carrier combined with fat, so they are more compatible with good health. If we should need more energy than usual, complex lipids can be made by the body from fat located in the storage areas.

Disorders of Lipids—How They Begin

Disorders of fat metabolism usually occur because plasma levels of individual fats have increased. For example, the cholesterol or triglyceride test levels are beyond the normal reference ranges. When these high levels are found, diet can be adjusted or medication prescribed to reduce them.

A More Complicated Problem

However, some disorders of the lipoproteins present complicated problems to a physician. They are classified as primary and secondary. Primary disorders are inherited, so they are called genetic or familial. These diseases are rare and not often encountered, so they will not be described here.

Secondary lipoprotein disorders can arise from:

- a diet in which excessive amounts of calories are consumed;
- diseases of body biochemistry such as diabetes, chronic kidney failure, and liver disease; or
- a hormone imbalance.

What Is Your Risk of Disease?

You know that VLDL contains a large amount of triglycerides and LDL contains a large amount of cholesterol. When excessive amounts of these fats accumulate inside of arteries, the walls become thick and start to harden. Atherosclerosis can develop over time.

Another danger is the formation of small clots (thrombi)

along blood vessel walls. The probability of this is increased when these plasma lipids have high test values. The original small clots become larger and eventually block the passage of blood in a blood vessel.

You can see why there is a correlation between high levels of bad cholesterols (VLDL and LDL) and the occurrence of cardiovascular (CV) disease. We can reverse this scenario and state that the higher the HDL level, the lower the risk of CV disease. This is the result of the protective action of HDL.

Your Doctor and Control

The reference range for cholesterol is 150–250 milligrams in each deciliter of serum. The recommended reference range for triglycerides is ten to ninety milligrams in each deciliter of serum. Various combinations of test values for lipids are used by clinical scientists and physicians to assess the status of fat metabolism in a patient. You see them in your clinical laboratory report calculated from your test results. The report will provide the formula used. This calculation will inform you of the risk factor you face as a result of your blood lipid profile. You may have a low risk or no risk at all.

Testing for Lipids

My brief description of the biochemical activity that goes on when we eat a fatty meal is good reason why test samples for lipids must be collected with care. Plasma lipid levels are affected by eating, changes in diet, smoking, and alcohol intake. If a patient is under stress, lipid test results may reflect this.

A blood sample for lipid testing is usually drawn after

twelve to fourteen hours of fasting with only water consumed. There are some current methods, however, that do not require fasting for the determination of LDL cholesterol. Your clinical laboratory will provide you with information about the method they use and whether it requires fasting. Electrophoresis and ultracentrifugation are used to separate the lipoproteins. Testing for lipids is also performed on the clinical chemistry autoanalyzers.

When a blood sample is drawn two or three hours after a meal, the plasma is cloudy because of the chylomicrons. When using traditional methods, if testing takes place with this sample of plasma, the result could be inaccurate. Instructions for sample collections should be followed closely, especially regarding fasting.

SECTION 9. PROTEINS

Important Proteins of the Blood

Plasma, the liquid portion of the blood after the cells are removed, is the transport system of the body. It contains various types of proteins that differ in their origin and function. Those connected with lipids have been discussed. The amount of protein in plasma depends on a balance between its formation in the liver and its use by the tissues.

A small fraction of proteins, the immunoglobulins, are not produced in the liver but are formed in the immune system, which protects us from infections. It is discussed in the immunology chapter.

What Is the "Total Protein"?

The two main protein groups in plasma are albumin and the globulins. A term used for the sum of these two is the *total protein* (TP), a test often requested. After an individual reaches fifty-five years of age, the quantity of total protein in plasma is constant. With aging, however, there is an increase in the globulin portion, but this is balanced by a decrease in albumin.

Origins of Protein

Protein enters the body in food that is made up of amino acids. Some of the amino acids needed to construct the serum proteins are made by our bodies. The other essential amino acids must be included in our food.

The Importance of Body Proteins

Proteins are a part of body tissues. Some of these are structural elements such as bone, tendons, cartilage, and muscle. All of our body cells that are not fat cells have some protein in them.

Other essential substances made up of protein are enzymes, hormones, antibodies, and coagulation factors. The immunoglobulin proteins respond to infection and help fight it. Proteins help in transporting hormones, vitamins, lipids, calcium, trace metals, and some drugs. Another important function is controlling fluid distribution in the body. Because they are important for homeostasis (a steady state of health), we must eat enough protein.

Albumin

Special Functions

Albumin is almost two-thirds of the total protein in normal plasma. It maintains the important osmotic pressure gradient in blood so that fluid carrying nutrients and wastes can move in and out of all body cells. This action is important for many reasons, but especially for electrolyte balance. Electrolytes are biochemical substances that carry electrical charges, which must be chemically balanced. They are especially important for the specialized cells of the kidneys.

During normal metabolism, the albumin is broken down into amino acids by body cells. These important protein building blocks are used to create other proteins that take part in tissue repair and body growth.

Some Additional Functions

Albumin carries hormones such as thyroxin, cortisol, and estrogen; minerals such as calcium, iron, and magnesium; and the important protein heme, a part of hemoglobin. Coumadin (which prevents the blood from clotting) and penicillin are two drugs that depend on albumin for transport.

Globulin: A Different Story

Some of the plasma globulins are similar to albumin in their activity. Others transport fats and substances that need fat to be digested such as vitamin A, vitamin D, and vitamin E.

The family of globulins comprise several fractions. The main ones are alpha$_1$ globulin, alpha$_2$ globulin, beta globulin, and gamma globulin. Gamma globulins are vital in fighting infection and counteracting inflammation. They maintain our immunity in the form of antibodies, which attack disease-causing bacteria and viruses. All of them have important functions in our everyday body metabolism. The alpha globulins are active in inflammatory disorders by minimizing damage to tissues. One of the beta globulins is transferrin, which transports iron from the iron stores in the body to the bone marrow for blood cell production.

Testing

Using Electrophoresis for Protein Identification

Individual plasma proteins can be separated, identified, and measured by electrophoresis. The protein particles in a patient's serum move on an agarose surface in the presence of an electric current. The speed and distance of this migration depend upon the molecular weight and the electric charge of the different proteins. They can be identified by the course they travel. Albumin and the different fractions of globulin are identified in this way.

Characteristic Changes in Disease

Disorders that result in abnormal amounts of serum protein generally show a decrease of the albumin fraction and an increase of globulin. The reference range of albumin is 3.2 to 4.5 grams in each deciliter of serum; for globulins, the reference range is 2.3 to 3.5 grams. The total protein, or albumin-plus-globulin value, is 6.0 to 7.8 grams per deciliter of serum.

Several disorders can be identified when specific patterns of protein electrophoresis show up in the test result. Typical patterns of individual fractions of (1) a normal plasma sample, (2) one found in chronic infection, (3) and one found in the presence of destructive lesions such as carcinoma are seen in the diagram.

Protein Disorders

AIDS

HIV invades T-lymphocytes with an unfavorable effect on the gamma globulins of the infected person. The patient's compromised defense system cannot fight the infections, resulting in chronic bacterial, viral, and fungal infections. More information about AIDS is found in the microbiology chapter.

Kidney Disease

The test for protein in the urine is part of urinalysis, routinely performed on all patients. It is an important test for preliminary assessment of kidney function. Protein in the urine specimen (proteinuria) signals chronic kidney disease before symptoms are experienced by a patient and before the blood urea nitrogen and creatinine tests show increased values.

Liver Disease

In a liver disorder, the coagulation proteins produced in the liver are decreased. Coagulation tests show abnormal results.

Plasma protein electrophoresis patterns

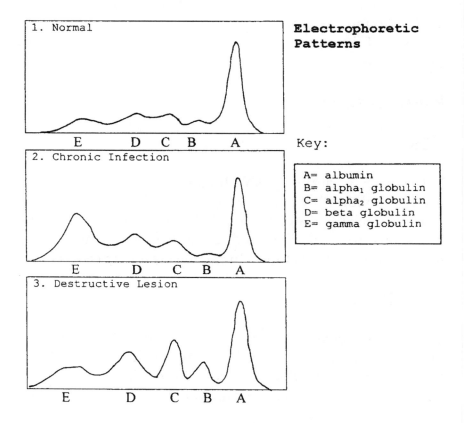

Electrophoretic Patterns

Key:

A= albumin
B= alpha₁ globulin
C= alpha₂ globulin
D= beta globulin
E= gamma globulin

The total protein (TP) and, in particular, albumin have abnormal levels in liver disorders.

Multiple Myeloma (MM)

This is a rare disease in which B-lymphocytes are transformed into plasma cells that produce excessive amounts of one of the globulins. Plasma cells play an important role in developing an immune response to invading bacteria and viruses.

This disorder is discovered by protein electrophoresis because there is an abnormal increase in one of the globulins. There are two types of MM—one in which the beta globulin is increased and the other in which the gamma globulin is increased.

The presence of an increased number of plasma cells, including abnormal ones discovered in a differential white blood cell count, is also diagnostic for multiple myeloma.

SECTION 10. THE THYROID GLAND

Homeostasis: A Steady State of Health

The endocrine system is a group of glands that produce hormones to keep the body in tune with our activity and the environment we live in. Some of the glands of this system are the adrenals and the pituitary (master gland), the thyroid, and the parathyroid glands, as well as the ovaries and testes. All are necessary for good health, but the thyroid hormones maintain our normal growth and metabolism.

The Gland That Sets the Pace

The thyroid is located in the neck in two connected sections, each lying on either side of the trachea (windpipe). Thyroxine, the hormone produced by this gland, speeds up our biochemical activity and influences cardiac output and heart rate. For children, a normally functioning thyroid is vital for growth, mental development, and sexual maturation.

Origin of the Hormone

Thyroxine formation begins with our intake of iodine, which the thyroid stores. Thyroxine is made in two forms—tetraiodothyronine (T_4) and triiodothyronine (T_3). Both are stored in thyroid tissue and secreted as they are needed.

Our general body metabolism, sometimes referred to as *basal metabolic rate* (BMR), can be defined as the rate at which energy is used by the body. This influences the oxygen we breathe and use. The result of this activity is the production of heat. All of this is regulated by the amount of T_4 and T_3 available. The presence of normal levels of the two thyroid hormones are important for adults and children.

The Importance of Iodine Intake

An adult eating a normal diet absorbs several hundred micrograms of iodine a day. The thyroid produces hormones from the iodine we consume utilizing the amino acid tyrosine. The success of the process depends on an adequate supply of iodide. Eating seafoods and adding iodized salt to our food provides us with sufficient iodide. About one-third of the iodine absorbed is taken up by the thyroid; the rest is excreted by the kidneys.

Our circulating blood normally contains T_4, with much smaller amounts of T_3. Most of T_4 and a small amount of T_3 are bound to a protein called thyroxine-binding globulin (TBG). It is by means of this protein that these hormones are transported in the blood.

T_4 and T_3 are also found in a free form in the bloodstream. Even though the amounts of free T_4 and T_3 in plasma are

Thyroid Hormone Secretion and Control

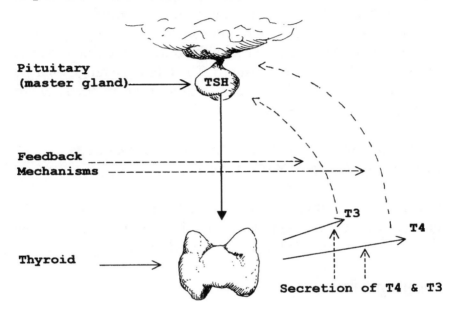

Pituitary (master gland)

TSH

Feedback Mechanisms

T3

T4

Thyroid

Secretion of T4 & T3

extremely small, testing for the free forms is important. The physician finds out their quantity in order to establish how well the thyroid and pituitary glands are functioning. You may recall that the latter is the "master gland," which exerts a certain amount of control over the others in the endocrine system.

Control of Thyroid Secretion

Plasma levels of free thyroxine are controlled by the pituitary. This gland, located at the base of the brain, keeps the levels of

T_4 and T_3 in the plasma within narrow limits. For example, when there is a low level of free T_4 and T_3, a thyroid-stimulating hormone (TSH) is released by the pituitary gland. This results in the release of thyroxine from the thyroid.

Conversely, when there is an excess of T_4 and T_3 in plasma, the release of TSH is held back by the pituitary so that the level of hormone in plasma is reduced. The reference range for T_4 is 4.5 to 13.0 micrograms in each deciliter of serum; for T_3, 60 to 220 nanograms per deciliter.

Disorders of the Thyroid Gland—Some Diseases Caused by Thyroid Malfunction

Diseases of the thyroid are classified on a functional basis. Overactivity of the gland is called hyperthyroidism. Low activity of the gland is known as hypothyroidism.

Hyperthyroidism

This disorder results when body tissues are exposed to excessive amounts of thyroxine. When the thyroid is overactive, symptoms such as a rapid heart rate, loss of weight, weakness, and being sensitive to heat are experienced.

The most common clinical syndrome connected with hyperthyroidism is Grave's disease. Another disorder causing hyperthyroidism is an increased growth of thyroid tissue, which is called hyperplasia. When there are tumors in the thyroid, hyperplasia may also be present.

Hypothyroidism

The condition resulting from lowered activity of the thyroid gland is hypothyroidism. In this disorder, there is a slowing down of thyroxine activity on the body tissues. Among the symptoms of hypothyroidism are hoarseness, sensitivity to cold, and the presence of dry skin and hair. The individual may also experience depression, a slow heartbeat, and muscle weakness.

The chronic form of hypothyroidism is called Hashimoto's disease, an autoimmune disorder that results in the destruction of thyroid tissue.

Causes for hypothyroidism are

- a decreased production of thyroxine by the gland,
- eating food with a low iodine content, and
- the harmful effect of drugs taken for other illnesses.

A goiter may develop in either hypothyroidism or hyperthyroidism. This is an enlargement of the thyroid, causing a swelling at the base of the neck. It is usually caused by a lack of iodine in the diet, so the treatment is iodine replacement therapy. However, in some cases, it may be necessary to remove the excess thyroid tissue surgically.

Pituitary Problems

A hidden cause for hypothyroidism is the malfunctioning of the master gland. If it releases decreased amounts of thyroid-stimulating hormone, the thyroid does not produce thyroxine, and hypothyroidism results. When this happens, the cause of the disorder is the pituitary gland and not the thyroid.

Testing

After a physician has performed a careful physical examination and has evaluated a patient's history, it may be evident that the thyroid is not functioning normally. Thyroid function tests are in two groups. There are those that establish that the gland is not functioning well. They include a TSH test and the serum concentration of total T_4 and total T_3. The second group is designed to tell us the cause of thyroid dysfunction. These tests include the detection of antibodies against the gland, throxine-binding globulin (TBG) measurements, and a sonography or biopsy of the gland. Your physician prefers one or two of these tests. Some of them make use of enzyme immunoassay or fluorescent immunoassay. This type of testing is discussed in the immunology/serology chapter of this book.

The reference ranges for these tests can be found on a clinical laboratory report when they are requested by your physician.

SECTION 11. ELECTROLYTES

Certain chemical elements in their smallest form carry electrical charges important for normal body functions. They are called electrolytes and are chemical ions carrying positive and negative charges in the blood and tissues. There must be an equilibrium, or balance, of these electrolyte charges between plasma and tissues. The disorders mentioned here affect the electrolyte values, causing an imbalance and resulting in serious illness.

Electrolytes and Body Function

Electrolytes are important for health because they play a leading role in maintaining water balance in the body. Examples of important ones are the sodium ion (Na^+), chloride ion (Cl^-), potassium ion (K^+), bicarbonate ion (HCO_3^-), and hydrogen ion (H^+). The electrical charges they carry enable them to move from blood to tissue cells and back again. As in our discussion of fat transport, water-based tissue fluids are essential for this exchange to take place. It is also important for the kidneys and lungs to function normally because they keep electrolytes in balance.

The Electrolyte Sodium

Sodium is especially important in controlling the water content of the body. Some causes for low plasma sodium levels are too much water intake; retention of water, as in heart failure or kidney disorders; and loss of sodium, along with fluid in prolonged diarrhea or excessive vomiting.

Some causes for high plasma sodium levels include loss of body water, leading to dehydration; excessive perspiring for extended periods of time; and some forms of diabetes.

Potassium

Another important electrolyte, potassium is an essential element in our food. Potassium ions help transmit impulses through the nervous system. As a result, if we have low levels of this ion in our blood, we may experience muscle weakness or heart irregularities.

Among the causes for low plasma potassium levels are diuretic medications that cause excessive loss of fluid and gastrointestinal loss of potassium in prolonged vomiting or diarrhea.

Among the causes for high plasma potassium levels are acute and chronic kidney failure, damage to body cells in high fever or in anemias when red blood cells are being destroyed, and consuming too many potassium supplements.

Additional Important Electrolytes

Other electrolytes include carbon dioxide and the bicarbonate ion, which play an important part in maintaining electrolyte balance in the lungs. Here the bicarbonate is changed biochemically to water and more carbon dioxide. Both of these by-products are eliminated when we breathe.

Hydrogen ions (H^+) are also a by-product of this reaction. They assist in maintaining the normal pH of blood. The pH of our blood must be maintained within a narrow range of 7.36 to 7.41. Kidney cells get rid of hydrogen ions by releasing them into the microscopic kidney tubules. From there they enter our urine, causing it to be slightly acid in pH. The physiological activity of the kidneys and lungs maintains a balance of electrolytes.

In summary, the by-products of these biochemical reactions and cellular secretions escape by way of the lungs as carbon dioxide and water. The kidneys help by getting rid of water and some of the ions to achieve a biochemical balance. But this is a simple explanation for a complex biochemical and biophysical process. By this time, you should understand the importance of healthy lungs and kidneys because they control the delicate balance of these indescribably small elements in our bodies.

Testing

Clinical chemistry panels provide you with a profile of your electrolytes. Mentioned at the beginning of this chapter, these tests may include the determination of sodium, potassium, chloride, and total carbon dioxide levels. The amount of carbon dioxide and oxygen—called blood gases—and a measurement of blood pH may also be requested. These are measured by sampling the arterial blood of patients, usually in a hospital setting.

In addition to the reasons I have mentioned for an imbalance of electrolytes, a physician may request them when certain medications are prescribed that alter their balance slightly. If this is the case, electrolytes are monitored closely with regular testing.

The reference values for these electrolytes appear on the clinical laboratory report when your physician requests them.

More information can be obtained in John Bernard Henry, *Clinical Diagnosis and Management by Laboratory Methods* (Philadelphia: W. B. Saunders, 2001).

chapter 5

Microbiology

SECTION 1. INTRODUCTION

This chapter is divided into six sections. First, there is a general description of some of the testing procedures performed in a microbiology laboratory. The next section discusses body systems and the microbes that normally inhabit them. The following four sections are about the characteristics of pathogenic bacteria, fungi, parasites, and viruses, respectively. The types of infections caused by each microbe are explained. The infections are arranged in alphabetical order.

Methods of diagnosis in the microbiology laboratory are very different from those of the other clinical laboratories that have been explored. In fact, bacteria and their relatives are so important that there are two laboratory disciplines that identify them—microbiology and immunology/serology. The first helps to identify the infecting microbes, and the second measures the effects of them on the host (the person infected). In

147

immunology, the response of the immune system in the form of antibodies is measured. In this way, harmful agents are tracked down, and the damage they have caused is assessed.

Good Bacteria and Bad Bacteria

Scientists have known for many years that there are beneficial microorganisms and harmful ones. The "good" ones are necessary for many things that go on in everyday life, such as cheese production and paint manufacturing. The yeast used for making bread is also a living microbe. It is fortunate for us that clinical laboratory scientists are more interested in studying and controlling "bad" bacteria, although we certainly appreciate the benefits of the "good" ones. The dangerous, disease-causing bacteria are called pathogens. They grow well inside the human body because of its favorable conditions, such as a warm environment and plenty of nourishment. When they invade the body and multiply, an infection results. Then, the infected individual is the "host" for the invading microorganism.

Colonization: A Different Partnership

The relationship between a microbe and a host in which neither one is benefited nor harmed is known as colonization. In simpler terms, bacteria survive in the body over the years as part of the normal flora. *Flora* refers to the variety of microorganisms that normally inhabit a certain area. In other words, microscopic organisms live in these places, causing no harm and, in some cases, doing good.

Opportunity for Pathogens to Survive

When they live in our bodies, pathogens are supplied with plenty of things that help their growth, such as oxygen, minerals, and vitamins. The harmful bacteria are able to live among the good ones and thrive in various places, such as the lungs, the sinuses, or the intestinal tract. But in these locations, the pathogens can cause serious diseases under certain conditions, usually when the body defenses are compromised. For instance, some strains of streptococcus (strep) live in the respiratory tract, as do staphylococci (staph). However, only a few members of these two groups cause serious infection when our defenses are weak.

The Language of Infection

In clinical terms, a *host* is a healthy human body that has been invaded by a disease-producing microorganism. A host's resistance to infection depends upon the bacteria's virulence. A virulent organism can resist the body's defenses and survive. In more specific terms, virulence is the extent to which pathogens can cause damage to the infected host. One way of hurting the host is when the bacteria produce a harmful toxin. This can be compared to a kind of poisoning.

How It All Starts

Infection is defined as the invasion and multiplication of harmful microorganisms in or on a host. Infectious bacteria enter a host when we inhale them, consume them in food or drink, or have contact with them on our internal or external body surfaces. After a week to several months, depending on the virulence of the bacteria and the person's defenses, a disease may develop. Once established, the bacteria are able to grow in the invaded tissue and produce toxins. This harms the host, who exhibits definite signs of developing illness such as inflammation, pain, heat, and swelling in the infected area. There may even be destruction of the invaded tissue.

The Picture of Repeated Infections

One infection following another compromises a host's defense mechanism. His immune system is unable to produce antibodies (or warriors) to fight the invaders. Even more disturbing is the fact that if large quantities of antibiotics are taken to kill the invader, the good bacteria are killed along with the bad. An unfavorable result is that the pathogen can become resistant to the antibiotics. Then, the pathogen multiplies and thrives despite the amount of antibiotic taken by a patient.

Infection and Public Health

Public health officials and epidemiologists use the terms *morbidity* and *mortality* to monitor and control disease outbreaks in communities. Epidemiologists find out the origin of a disease and when and where it occurs. They depend on the clinical laboratory to produce information needed to develop statistics about disease patterns.

Morbidity means having a disease. *Morbidity rate* is used by public health officials to describe the proportion or number of people with a particular disease during a given year in a certain population. For example, in 1986, there were one million people in a certain country who where admitted to hospitals with infections.

Mortality rate is another term commonly used by health officials. It refers to a ratio of the total number of deaths to the total population of a given community. It is expressed as the number of deaths in one thousand or ten thousand people.

Classifying Bacteria

There is a lengthy scientific classification system for all living organisms. Bacteria are among the most primitive of living forms, but scientists have given names to them, too. In the final part of a long scientific name, there are two words. The first word is the genus, which is capitalized. The second word is the species, which is not capitalized. An example is the scientific name for humans, *Homo sapiens*. When we use this classification method in referring to the bacterium *Staphylococcus aureus*, the genus is *Staphylococcus*, and the species is *aureus*.

Microbiologists Solving Mysteries

When clinical laboratory scientists perform testing in a microbiology laboratory, they examine and grow organisms from specimens so that the bacteria causing an illness can be identified. It is important to identify a pathogen soon after it has entered the body to minimize its harm to the host.

After the pathogen is known, a test is performed to find out which antibiotic can kill it or inhibit its growth. This is called an antimicrobial susceptibility test. The name of the bacteria causing the illness is known, so now the antibiotics that could kill it are tested with the bacteria. Then, we observe which antibiotic inhibits their growth. This one is used to treat the patient.

Technology today allows us to find an effective antibiotic in hours. This is a definite advantage for a physician who learns the identity of the bacteria that is infecting her patient and the antibiotic that can eliminate it in time to relieve illness.

Before explaining the traditional manner in which bacteria are identified, it is important to mention one of the many innovations in microbiology. A sensor has been devised that gives the cells that provide immunity against viruses or bacteria the ability to become luminescent in the presence of these invaders. This helps clinical scientists identify them.

Getting Started with Testing

In a microbiology laboratory, there is a step-by-step process of testing. In the beginning, a patient sees a physician when symptoms suggest an infection. A physical examination leads to possible causes. A sample of a discharge or body fluid or a swab with surface tissue on it taken from the area of infection is collected. These specimens are used to grow (culture) the suspected pathogen. A clinical laboratory used by your physician provides a specimen container and instructions for collecting and transporting it. This is important because the condition and quantity of the specimen will determine the reliability of the test result.

Tracing a Specimen in the Laboratory

In the laboratory, information on the request form is entered into a computer and "bar coded," much like supermarket bar codes. All precautions for infection control are followed by a clinical scientist in handling and preparing a small amount of specimen for microscopic examination. These safeguards may include wearing gloves, protective clothing, and a mask and using a biological safety cabinet in which to carry out the tests. Clinical scientists use sterile technique in all procedures in a microbiology laboratory, and this is called universal precautions.

Testing Procedures

The Dry Mount

When it is received by a clinical scientist, a portion of the specimen is examined directly. This may involve making smears of the material on glass slides and staining them with dyes to show the yeast, bacteria, white blood cells, and red blood cells. The name for this is a dry mount.

In this preparation, a smear is made of the infectious material on a glass slide. This is carefully accomplished by means of a hand-held instrument called a loop, which delivers a drop of fluid. It is made of durable, disposable plastic. There is a pencil-shaped handle with a four-inch extension of fine wire or plastic at the front end. The wire may be shaped like a needle or a small loop.

The Gram Stain

Once the smear of infectious material is carefully dried over a heater, a series of dyes applied to the slide results in some bacteria staining purple and others red. This stain is used routinely in microbiology. It is called a Gram stain after the man who invented it in the late 1800s. A preliminary identification of the pathogen is made when this preparation is viewed in the microscope.

Some bacteria take on a red color and are considered Gram negative. Others take on a purple color and are considered Gram positive. The Gram stain gives us a clue as to the identification, but the shape now visible also helps. For example, we may see Gram-negative cocci or Gram-positive bacilli. The family of pathogens could be identified at this point, which helps the bacteriologist pick the culture media to be inoculated in order to grow the bacteria for further testing.

Presumptive Identification Can Be Made

In case of urgency to treat a very sick patient, a dry mount is used to identify the bacteria quickly. The reporting of the pathogen at this point is called a presumptive report. The usual procedure is to culture the pathogen to confirm its identification. The presumptive report is used only when a severe infection is suspected. Knowing the probable invader, a physician is informed of the appropriate antibiotic and begins a course of treatment.

Culturing a Pathogen

By now you are aware that bacteria cannot be seen with the human eye. Microscopes are used to magnify them 950 to 1000 times so they become visible to us. Clinical scientists observe the shape and size of bacteria when they are Gram stained to initially identify them. Biochemical requirements of pathogens are used to find out more about them. For example, some bacteria need certain nutrients to grow. The most common ones are agar gel and various kinds of meat broth. Agar is a gelatinlike substance that bacteria prefer. The pathogenic bacteria grow better on agar that contains blood.

When the suitable medium is selected for good growth of this bacteria or fungus, it is inoculated with a small portion of the specimen using the sterile loop. The media containers used for growth are usually petri dishes and sometimes large test tubes.

How Does This Garden Grow?—Incubation of Media That Has Been Inoculated

After the culture medium has been inoculated with a portion of the specimen, it is placed in a large commercial incubator, which provides the best temperature and conditions for maximum bacterial growth. Each type of bacteria takes a different length of time to grow into colonies. The physical characteristics of the colonies, the nutrients present in the culture medium, and the biochemical requirements for growth all help identify the pathogen.

Observing Growth and Reaction of the Organism

After twenty-four hours, petri plates and test tubes inoculated with the specimen are examined for growth. The bacteria grow into colonies on the agar gel that can be observed. For example, the color of the growth at the center or edge of a colony provides valuable information. Whether the colonies are smooth and shiny or dull and dry is also important for identification.

A Special Identification System

Some enterobacteria that are intestinal tract inhabitants require more intense study to find the invader species. A drop or two of the pure culture is transferred to an identification system, which is used to find out the differential biochemical reactions of the pathogen. This system in test-kit form consists of different biochemicals such as dextrose, hydrogen sulfide, indole, citrate, lysine, and urease, to name a few. Each species within the genus of *Enterobacteria* has typical reactions in this test kit. After a period of incubation, the test results are observed and a positive identification of the species can be made.

Some currently used systems allow the infecting bacteria to be identified in a shorter time than traditional methods. They make use of an enzyme reaction in which the microbes take part. The resulting color from this interaction identifies the bacteria.

Looking at Them up Close

You realize by this time that finding and identifying microorganisms is not an easy task. Up to this point, we have cultured them, nurtured them, and observed them from afar. When viewing them with a microscope, we can see that each species has a different shape. Some are tiny spheres called cocci that may be in pairs (diplococci) or in rows that resemble a string of beads (streptococci). Other cocci are in clumps, like a small bunch of grapes.

Other bacteria are rod shaped. These are called bacilli; a single one is a bacillus. The rods may be long and thin like *Mycobacteria*; one member of this genus causes tuberculosis. Another bacillus may be short and fat like *Clostridia*; a member of this genus causes botulism, or food poisoning. There are also long, twisted spirals that are flexible. Other spirals are stiff and are called spirochetes. *Treponema pallidum* is a spirochete that causes syphilis.

The cocci cannot move about, but some of the rod-shaped bacteria do move in tissue and cell fluid by means of fine, hair-like structures on their surfaces. Some spiral bacteria move by means of long, whiplike structures attached at one end that rotate. All bacteria need fluid or moist conditions in which to live. When conditions are not favorable for growth, some bacteria go into a resting stage and change into spores. This inactive capsule form cannot be penetrated by ordinary means and preserves bacteria until the environment is suitable again for growth.

SECTION 2. BODY SYSTEMS AND INFECTIONS

What Is Normal Bacterial Flora?

From an early age, we live with microbes surrounding us in the air and water and on all surfaces. You may recall that the human body has certain areas that are permanently populated with good bacteria. For example, the large intestine has a variety of beneficial bacteria. This is considered a "normal flora" of bacteria that thrive and cause no harm.

There are sterile areas in the body as well. They normally have no bacteria except during infection. If bacteria are suspected of being in sterile areas, your doctor collects a specimen for culture so that the invader can be identified.

In the following, the normal flora of various body systems is presented. A short description of the pathogens that could invade each system follows.

A. Our Breathing Apparatus

The upper respiratory tract has a variety of microorganisms. Some of the strains in our mouth and on our teeth are of the *Staphylococcus*, *Streptococcus*, and *Enterobacteria*. The abbreviations *Staph* and *Strep* will be used in this book for the first two genera. The prefix *entero-* refers to a group of organisms that live mainly in the intestines. In the throat, nose, and sinuses, *Strep pneumoniae*, *Strep pyogenes*, and *Neisseriae menigitidis* are found. *Proteus*, *Hemophilus influenzae*, and *Fusobacterium* inhabit the throat and tonsils. Keep in mind that some of these members are pathogens.

The sterile areas are the larynx (voice box), trachea (windpipe), bronchi, and bronchioles. Bronchi and bronchioles are breathing tubes of different diameters located in the lungs to carry air in and out of the body.

Infection Takes Hold

When we are ill, usually during cold weather, acute infections will result in bronchitis, an inflammation of the bronchial tree. This problem is experienced by people of all ages. The infection is usually caused by adenoviruses and the influenza virus in combination with *Strep pneumoniae*, *Strep pyogenes*, *Hemophilus influenzae*, and *Mycoplasma pneumoniae*.

Two particularly infectious bacteria are *Hemophilus influenzae* and *Bordetella pertussis*. Even though their presence has been curtailed by vaccines during infancy and childhood, they occasionally cause serious illness.

Some Types of Respiratory Infections

The following alphabetical listing describes some of the respiratory infections we can encounter.

Anthrax bacillus—anthrax (*Bacillus anthracis*). Anthrax, an infectious disease caused by this bacteria, occurs in hoofed animals and can infect humans. Although anthrax is rare in the United States, a recent finding of spores in the mail in various locations has brought it to the forefront. Prior to this incident, if we were to look at a history of the disease, we would find that it has been controlled in animals in the United States for many years.

When conditions are not suitable for growth, some bacteria change to a resting stage, the spore form. Anthrax spores increase in number in the soil. Animals become infected when they graze. Humans are exposed to this bacillus when they contact these animals. Usually the spores are transmitted to humans by animal products like wool and hair. The part of the body involved is usually the skin, rarely the lungs and intestinal tract. The different forms of human anthrax infection are cutaneous (through the skin), inhalation, and intestinal.

When the means of entry is the skin, a small reddish lesion appears in one to five days after contact with the infectious material. The lesion develops into a hemorrhagic site that eventually ruptures and becomes a painless ulcer. The infection may spread to the lymphatic vessels and nodes, which may result in swollen lymph nodes. In some instances, the bloodstream is infected.

In the inhalation form of the infection, the spores cause cold symptoms and difficulty in breathing. A severe infection of the lymph glands in certain areas of the body follows. This type of infection is discovered by chest x-rays.

The third route of entry is the gastrointestinal tract when spores are taken in while eating contaminated food. This causes inflammation of the intestinal tract with nausea, loss of appetite, fever, and diarrhea.

In all these examples, the spores have found suitable conditions in the body for them to change into the bacterial form. They become active harmful pathogens again.

Early treatment of anthrax infection is important. A vaccine is available for use in humans. The diagnostic testing for this infection is found in the immunology/serology chapter.

Beta-hemolytic Streptococci—Strep throat. Infection with these cocci occurs by way of the respiratory tract when we are in personal contact with infected individuals. These organisms are members of a division of the beta-hemolytic strep family called Group A. This serious infection at first causes an acute inflammation of the throat (pharyngitis). Medical attention should be sought for prompt treatment so that serious complications can be avoided. Scarlet fever is also caused by this microbe. Serious disorders that can result from neglecting a strep infection are rheumatic fever, endocarditis (a heart muscle infection), and chronic or acute kidney disease.

The toxin these bacteria produce when they infect us allows clinical scientists to identify them as the invader. The toxin, streptolysin O, is released into the tissues and stimulates the production of antibodies called antistreptolysin, which neutralizes the toxin and helps fight the infection. The test for these antibodies is described in the immunology/serology chapter.

Bordetella pertussis—**whooping cough**. *B. pertussis* causes a respiratory infection commonly known as whooping cough. It is passed from person to person by coughing. When antibodies are produced in a new host, the antigens on the surface of the bacterial cell that caused the antibody production change. By doing this, the bacterium can survive longer because the victim must produce new antibodies each time the antigens change. This makes it difficult to cure a patient.

The disease produces a staccato cough known as a "whooping" cough, which is often followed by vomiting. A diagnosis can be made by a physician with these two observations. The infection can last for months. A vaccine is used during infancy to prevent the disease. A molecular biotechnology test, namely, polymerase chain reaction (PCR), can be used for a diagnosis.

Haemophilus influenzae—**the flu**. *H. influenzae* is a virulent organism that can cause rapidly progressive infections in the respiratory tract. An ear infection may follow the respiratory problem. In untreated infections of long duration, it can lead to meningitis, an inflammation of the membranes surrounding the brain and spinal cord.

Infants and young children are most susceptible to this contagious disease. Siblings under six are given a vaccine that causes them to have an antibody response that protects them.

Legionella—Legionnaires' disease. In the summer of 1976, there was an outbreak of pneumonia at an American

Legion convention in Philadelphia. The authorities did not know the cause. The microbe responsible was isolated and identified the next year and named *Legionella pneumophilia*. The illness was called Legionnaire's disease. The microbe had lived in the hotel's air conditioning system.

This organism is another invader of the respiratory tract. It is a well-known pathogen that finds a home in air conditioning units that are not properly maintained. Exposure to pathogens of this group causes pneumonia in adults.

Mycobacterium tuberculosis—**tuberculosis.** Different bacteria of the genus *Mycobacterium* can attack the lungs, lymph nodes, skin, or gastrointestinal tract. For example, *Mycobacterium leprae* attacks the skin, causing leprosy. The tubercle bacillus we are discussing attacks the lungs. Most of these microbes are Gram-positive rods, but some of them when Gram stained do not take on the dye well and are difficult to see with the microscope. The problem is solved by using special procedures such as the acid-fast stain. It is strongly positive when these bacteria are present in the specimen. When these slender, rose-colored, acid-fast bacilli are found in sputum or lung tissue, a diagnosis can be made.

Tuberculosis is a highly communicable disease. There may be outbreaks of it when people are confined or in crowded living conditions. People who are most likely to become infected are those who have poor nutrition or an immune system that is below par. If a patient has a chronic debilitating disease, the bacillus can invade and establish itself. When an infection is confirmed, treatment is provided with antituberculin drugs.

The primary site of infection with M. *tuberculosis* is the lungs; therefore, sputum samples are used for clinical laboratory diagnosis. The specimen should be expressed early in the morning into a sterile collection device.

After the diagnosis has been established, treatment is begun. A test for sputum examination is conducted at one-week intervals. In this way, the effectiveness of medication can be monitored.

Neisseria meningitidis—**meningitis.** The bacteria of the *Neisseria* genus are small cocci that appear in pairs. They are Gram negative, so the pairs of cocci are deep pink when viewed with a microscope. The infection in adolescents and adults causes cerebrospinal meningitis. Meningitis is an inflammation of the membranes covering the brain and spinal cord.

The first symptoms are a frontal headache, followed by a stiff neck and rigidity in the cervical spine area. The patient may have had an upper respiratory infection with a laryngitis or pharyngitis. Vomiting and pain in the joints may be present later in the infection as the acute stage develops. In these late stages, respiratory distress, shock, or a rash may be present.

When these organisms are found in the cerebrospinal fluid of the patient there is strong suspicion that meningitis is present. A definite diagnosis is made when N. *meningitidis* is observed growing in culture. Positive serological tests for the bacteria further confirm the diagnosis.

Parts of the bacteria called antigens have been used to develop vaccines for the infection. Antigens are protein substances on the surface of the organism. When the vaccine is administered to the infected person, the illness is less severe.

B. The Gastrointestinal Tract

The large intestine harbors many bacteria, including *Staph epidermidis* and *Staph aureus* and various species of *Streptococcus*, *Corynebacteria*, *Mycobacteria*, *Clostridia*, *Actinomycetes*, and *Enterobacteria*. When peritonitis or abscesses in the abdomen occur, the causative agents are a mixed group of bacteria. Peritonitis is an infection of the abdominal cavity and one of the serious consequences of a ruptured appendix or bowel.

The usually sterile areas of the gastrointestinal tract are the esophagus and stomach. Bacteria that we consume with food do not survive in the stomach's acid secretions. Additional sterile areas are the small intestine, the liver, and the gallbladder.

Clostrudium botulinum—**botulism food poisoning.** Botulism is a type of bacterial food poisoning. This classic disease is the result of consuming the potent toxin produced by these bacteria in contaminated food. The toxin acts on our nervous system, resulting in an acute, descending paralysis. The pathogen is identified by culturing the organism and by testing its differential biochemical reactions. When a microbiology laboratory is certain that *Clostridium botulinum* is the infecting agent, a local public health laboratory or the Centers for Disease Control and Prevention must be notified.

Helicobacter pylori—**gastritis or ulcer.** These bacteria have been found in the unfriendly environment of the stomach. The stomach is normally highly acidic. Oddly, the bacteria thrive there. When present and surviving, *H. pylori* causes inflammation and ulceration of the stomach wall. There is some evidence that this microbe is associated with ulcers in the stomach and duodenum (small intestine).

There are more rapid methods for detecting *H. pylori* than a culture. One is the CLO test, which takes advantage of the high urease activity of the bacteria. Another is the urea breath test (UBT). A polymerase chain reaction test has also been developed.

A traditional serological blood test detects antibodies to *H. pylori*. These methods include an agglutination test and an enzyme immunoassay.

Salmonella **and** ***Shigella/Escherichia*** **species—diarrhea.** These species are included in the family of *Enterobacteria*. When infected, they cause severe diarrhea and even hemorrhage in the large intestine (colon). When this happens, blood can be found in the stool. This condition is called colitis, an inflammation of the colon to the point of bleeding.

The early symptoms of a *Shigella* infection include the presence of a fever, diarrhea with a watery stool, and cramping abdominal pain. In *salmonella* infections, the same symptoms are present, along with nausea and vomiting. A severe infection can cause *salmonella* to invade the bloodstream.

Escherichia coli Infections

E. coli is found in many types of infections—including urinary tract infections, wound infections, pneumonia in patients with a compromised immune system, and meningitis in newborns. It can invade practically every organ. Some strains of *E. coli* cause traveler's diarrhea, and others invade epithelial cells of the intestine, causing dysentery. Serological testing is used in the clinical laboratory to differentiate between the different strains of the organism.

Any of these pathogens of *Enterobacteria* can enter the body when we eat contaminated food or when we drink water or milk containing traces of human or animal urine and feces. It is important to seek medical attention when an infection by these organisms is suspected. The primary symptom is dehydration caused by the loss of fluid from prolonged diarrhea.

C. Genitourinary Tract

This system includes the reproductive organs and urinary tract. The microorganisms that are normally present on external genitals and usually do not cause disease are some *Staphylococcus* species, some strains of *Streptococci* and *Enterococci*, and the yeast *Candida albicans*. Certain species of these organisms can cause sexually transmitted diseases. The sterile areas are the kidneys, ureters, bladder, and the internal female and male genital tracts.

An Infection Caused by Normal Flora

Gardnerella vaginalis can sometimes cause an infection, although small numbers are normally present in the vagina. In women, fecal material containing *Staphylococcus* and *Enterobacteria* from the area surrounding the anus can produce infections of the urinary tract or genital tract.

Sexually Transmitted Infections

Venereal infections produce specific lesions of the genitals that can be recognized by a physician. At that time, a preliminary identification of the infecting microbe takes place. As a group, these infections are called sexually transmitted diseases

166

(STDs). Some of these are chlamydia, syphilis, gonorrhea, herpes simplex, candida, trichomonas, and human papilloma virus (HPV).

Etiology of Sexually Transmitted Diseases

The cold and the flu are the most common infections, but sexually transmitted diseases are becoming more common. There are thirty-five to fifty different kinds of STDs. A large percentage of them occur in people younger than twenty-five. Most people do not develop symptoms immediately after infection, but they are still contagious. To add to the problem, some current strains of these infecting microbes resist treatment.

The STDs That Deserve Our Attention

Sexually transmitted diseases are caused by several pathogenic bacteria. The most serious ones involve the bacteria *Treponema pallidum*, which causes syphilis, followed by *Neisseria gonorrhea* and *Chlamydia*.

The viral STDs include the genital human papilloma virus, genital herpes simplex, the hepatitis B virus, cytomegalovirus, and HIV/AIDS. A parasite that causes an STD is *Trichomonas vaginalis*. These viral and parasitic infections are discussed in the virus and parasite sections of this chapter.

The Damage Caused by STDs

The effects of these infections are devastating to women and men. During the course of these disorders, there may be acute or chronic pain. Women can develop pelvic inflammatory disease (PID), which results in internal organ damage and may end in sterility. Cervical cancer can develop when there is long-term infection in women, and genital cancer may occur in men. In addition, some infections are passed on by the mother to her offspring at birth. For example, the HIV and herpes infection of a mother can infect her newborn infant.

Some Diseases of the Genitourinary Tract

Chlamydia. The genus *Chlamydia* contains several species that can cause STD infections in humans. *Chlamydia trachomatis* is a human pathogen that causes urethritis (inflammation of the urethra) in men and cervicitis (inflammation of the cervix) in women. It is the most common sexually transmitted bacterial pathogen.

Neisseria gonorrhea—**gonorrhea.** This pathogen causes an acute inflammation of the urethra and a discharge in men. After infection occurs, symptoms appear in one to seven days. In women, the infection causes an inflammation of the cervix with a vaginal discharge. There may be lower abdominal pain and, in some women, abnormal bleeding. Without treatment, the infection may ascend into other sexual organs. Sometimes these gonococcal infections do not have accompanying symptoms. Therefore, it is important that people at high risk for STDs are screened periodically to prevent the unknowing spread of this pathogen.

Treponema pallidum—**syphilis.** This organism causes syphilis, which can be transmitted by several routes, such as direct sexual contact, introduction into the bloodstream by shared needles, or direct contact with infectious lesions.

There are three distinct stages of the disease. First, a painless lesion at the site of infection in the female or male genital region appears. The second stage results in a skin rash, lymph node enlargement, a fever, and lethargy. In this stage the liver and central nervous system become involved. The last stage results in inflammatory lesions in various tissues and organs, including the heart, joints, and nervous system. This is a devastating illness if neglected and allowed to enter the later stages.

D. The Integument or Skin

Different microorganisms are present on our skin as a result of the places in which we live and work. The outer ear canal is included when we consider the skin area. Some of the harmless species of *Staphylococci*, *Corynebacteria*, *Propionibacteria*, and *Mycobacteria* inhabit the skin under ordinary conditions. Some yeasts also live on our skin. The middle and inner ear are usually sterile.

Some Infections of the Skin

- *Staph aureus*—boil. This organism causes skin boils.
- *Staph epidermidis*—acne. This is the causative agent in pimples and acne.
- *Strep pneumoniae* and *Pseudomonas aeruginosa*—ear infection. Either of these organisms can cause external ear infections, especially after swimming.

The Middle and Inner Ear

The middle and inner ear can become infected when there is a generalized illness of a debilitating nature. The microorganisms that could cause infections under these conditions are *Staph aureus*, *Strep pneumoniae*, *Strep pyogenes*, or *Pseudomonas aeruginosa*. When *Hemophilus influenzae* is present in the throat or nasopharynx, it too can infect the sterile areas of the ear.

When a host has experienced repeated infections and the immune system is weakened, *Staph aureus* can cause inflammation of heart tissue (endocarditis) and lung abscesses.

Diseases Involving Breaks in the Skin Barrier

***Borrelia burgdorferi*—Lyme disease.** Lyme disease is another infectious disease caused by a spiral-shaped bacterium called a spirochete. Humans become infected from tick bites when living in the Northeastern and Midwestern United States. The tick spends part of its life cycle in the white-tailed deer's fur. If the spirochetes are inside the tick they can be transmitted into human skin through a bite. As the bacteria grow in the skin, an expanding lesion appears where the victim was bitten. Over time, the spirochetes can move from the primary site to major organs of the body. It is most important to seek medical advice soon after a suspicious lesion is seen on the limbs or anywhere on the body.

***Clostridium tetani*—tetanus.** Tetanus results from an infection caused by the bacteria *Clostridium tetani*. If you step on a rusty nail or piece of glass, inflicting a wound, and spores of this microbe are present, they can cause a serious infection. The bacteria produces a toxin that causes voluntary muscles of the body to contract. One of the first areas to be affected is the face. The term *lock jaw* has been used to describe this condition.

Spores of this organism are widely distributed in the soil and in water. It is important to obtain medical treatment immediately after experiencing a deep cut or puncture wound caused by dirty or rusty objects. A vaccine protects us even when we receive it only every five to ten years.

Rabies virus—rabies. Rabies is a virus infection caused by a break in the skin barrier when we are bitten by a rabid animal. A rare infection in the United States, rabies is discussed fully in the virus section of this chapter.

West Nile virus. This is spread by the bite of an infected mosquito. Various animals, including horses and many types of birds, can become infected. It is rare for humans to acquire this infection. The best protection is to avoid being bitten by infected mosquitoes. This infection is described fully in the virus section of this chapter.

Can Antibiotics Help?

Many bacteria today have become resistant to antibiotics. For example, some strains of *Enterobacteria* have developed resistance to cephalothin, ampicillin, colistin, polymyxins, tetracyclines, and nitrofurantoins.

Other genera of bacteria have also proved to be resistant to antimicrobial agents. Some members of the genus *Staphylococcus* and *Strep pneumoniae* are known to be resistant to certain antibiotics. If antibiotics are used when not absolutely necessary, more bacteria can become resistant.

That is why the results of the antimicrobial susceptibility tests performed in a microbiology laboratory are important. They ensure us that the right medication is provided to cure the patient of the existing infection.

SECTION 3. MYCOLOGY—THE STUDY OF FUNGI

Another branch of microbiology is the study of fungi (fungus in the singular).

A. What Are They and What Do They Look Like?

Fungi are successful living organisms, as they exist everywhere in nature. We can observe these organisms visually, and we can examine them closely with a microscope. As part of the energy cycle, when fungi are present in compost, they help decompose matter. Most fungi infections are not contagious. We acquire them through exposure to a source in nature where the fungus lives.

When we study their "form," we are learning about their *morphology*. Fungi can exist in two forms—as one-celled or many-celled organisms. They also take on many shapes. We classify them as yeasts or molds on the basis of their morphology.

The Yeast Form

The yeast form is defined as a cell that reproduces by budding. This means that a yeast cell pinches off a portion of itself, or a "bud," to produce a daughter cell. When these organisms are grown in a petri dish on special agar culture media, they produce circular, pasty, moist-looking colonies. Variations in the color and texture of these colonies help identify the yeast causing the infection.

The Mold Form

The morphology of molds directly contrasts with the yeast forms. Their structure is made up of cells with many different shapes. The colonies produce filaments called *hyphae* that can be seen when viewed with a microscope. These hyphae interweave to form a network of filaments. When we look at a mold on culture media, we see fuzzy-looking colonies growing on special types of agar. We refer to the ability of fungi to thrive in two distinctly different forms as dimorphic.

The families of fungi are numerous, but only a few cause disease in humans. When our immune system is functioning normally, we can resist infections with these organisms. However, if the immune system is compromised by repeated infections, the fungi that are not ordinarily pathogens can cause illness.

B. Culture Methods

Culture methods used by clinical scientists to identify fungi are similar to those used for bacteria. However, the types of agar and broth used to culture them contain extra carbohydrates, especially sugars. The nutrients that fungi like are added to the culture medium. Usually, antibiotics are added to the media to prevent bacteria from growing. Bacterial growth would prevent a pure culture of the fungus causing the infection.

A Closer Look at These Fungi

Clinical scientists observe growing fungi colonies on agar to gain valuable information. If we want to examine them with a microscope, wet mounts or dry mounts are prepared from samples of a growing colony.

C. Types of Fungal Infections

There are two pathways for these infections to occur. Pathogens can belong to the family of superficial organisms that live on and in skin layers, including the nails and hair. The other path for infection involves our internal body systems. These pathogens are called deep systemic fungi. They cause serious medical problems.

1. Infection by Superficial Fungi

This type of fungus can occur on the skin, covering all parts of the body, and can be easily discovered and treated. Several are described here.

Microsporum canis—**ringworm.** An example of superficial or skin infection is ringworm. We can become infected by close contact with pets—like dogs and cats that carry it. The skin lesions in animals result in the loss of fur. In humans, the microorganism invades skin and hair. Lesions can occur on the upper body, neck, face, and limbs. Infected children and adults can have hair loss.

Candida—**yeast infection.** A yeast form that infects the skin are members of the *Candida* family, which can cause skin and nail diseases.

Candida albicans is a common organism that lives on the skin and mucous membranes. It can become a serious infection when present in the oral cavity, trachea, bronchi, and even the gastrointestinal tract. In the female genital region, it causes vulvovaginitis, an inflammation of the vagina and external genitals. These conditions can be treated.

A systemic infection with other members of the *Candida* family is relatively rare. However, when infection is system-wide, it can cause a serious illness, such as endocarditis (inflammation of heart tissue) and meningitis.

2. The Deep Systemic Fungi

Blastomyces dermatitidis—**blastomycosis.** Among the deep systemic fungi causing serious illness is *Blastomyces dermatitidis*, which causes North American blastomycosis. The fungus is believed to enter the host by way of the respiratory tract and then spread into the lungs. The disease can also cause skin inflammation.

Histoplasma capsulatum—**histoplasmosis.** This is a fungus that causes histoplasmosis in the eastern and central regions of the United States. The organism has been isolated from soil where there are dried droppings of chickens, birds, and bats. The pathogen enters the body by means of the respiratory tract. From there, spontaneous disease can occur in humans, dogs, rats, or cattle. A small number of those infected by the fungus develop a progressive, debilitating disease.

Coccidioides immitis. This fungus causes coccidioidomycosis, an endemic disease of the San Joaquin Valley in Arizona and western Texas. The organism lives in the soil and enters the host by means of the respiratory tract. Lesions develop in the lungs and bronchial tree that can be healed with treatment. Early discovery of the infection and prompt treatment is successful in halting the disease.

Although these fungus infections are rare in humans, it is to your advantage to know about them. Armed with this knowledge, you can take necessary precautions in situations where they may be a threat.

SECTION 4. PARASITES THAT CAUSE DISEASE

A. What Is a Parasite?

A parasite is an organism that lives in or on a host and may or may not harm the host. Parasites represent a large group of microbes that can be found in all parts of the world. When we are infected with a parasite, the resulting relationship benefits the parasite but can potentially harm the host's health. Those that cause localized damage to a host's tissues are regarded as pathogens.

B. What Are Some Characteristics?

The Life Cycles of a Parasite

Parasites have prolonged and complicated life cycles. By *life cycles* we mean that parasites go through different physical stages of development as they live in different hosts. Each parasite has its own life cycle, and takes on different physical forms as it progresses. Phases include an infective stage, a resting stage in the form of a cyst, an adolescent stage, and an adult stage. The infected host becomes the victim in any of these stages.

Some Baffling Characteristics of Parasites

You now know that parasites take on a variety of forms while maturing. To complicate matters further, a parasite can be a one-celled or a many-celled creature. The great diversity of these organisms is evident when we notice that they span a biological spectrum that includes microscopic organisms at one end and visible parasites, such as roundworms or tapeworms, at the other. The microscopic one-celled organisms are referred to as protozoa. Some of the one-celled creatures have hairlike structures that they use while moving around in body fluids.

Entry of the Parasite

After they enter a host, parasites usually live near a food supply, such as the blood vessels or the intestines. The manner of entering a "residence" is different for almost every type of parasite. Some enter our bodies when we eat food or drink water containing the infective stage of the parasite. An example is the amoeba, a one-celled parasite that causes amoebic dysentery. We can be infected with it when eating unwashed vegetables in tropical climates.

Other parasites enter the body when an insect carrier called a vector injects the parasite into our skin. This invader enters underlying tiny capillary blood vessels, then the bloodstream. For example, a certain species of mosquito can carry protozoan forms of the malaria parasite. When an infected mosquito stings us, the parasite is injected into our skin and enters our blood.

The disease schistosomiasis enters the host differently. It has a stage that burrows into the skin. This parasite is from the species *schistosoma*, and the burrowing forms are called cercaria. This is an intermediate stage of development that lives freely in fresh water in tropical climates. They can enter our skin when wading in shallow pools where the parasite lives.

Establishing a Home after Gaining Entry

After entering the body, the parasites may not survive to establish a permanent home. There must be favorable conditions. For example, there should be a sufficient number of parasites for the invasion, and they must have staying power, or virulence. Finally, and most importantly, a weak immune response by the host is essential.

C. The Testing Process

Testing to Prove the Presence of a Parasite

The most common specimen used to investigate the presence of a parasite is the stool. A small portion of the specimen is placed in fixatives such as 10 percent formalin (formaldehyde) or polyvinyl alcohol (PVA) to preserve it. This portion can then be examined microscopically as we search for both the parasite's eggs (ova) and the active parasite. An experienced clinical laboratory scientist who is a microbiologist discovers the parasite and reports the findings. Then, treatment is started.

D. Avoiding Infection Is Vital

In the following discussion, the pathogenic parasites reviewed are the most common on a worldwide basis. These parasites can infect us easily when we are not aware of how they are transmitted. Therefore, knowledge about them is in our best interest, especially in view of the extensive world travel today. Infection can occur quickly and without warning. It is to your advantage to know how and where you can become infected. Then, the risk of acquiring the parasite can be avoided.

SECTION 5. PROTOZOA—ONE-CELLED PARASITES

Entamoeba histolytica—**amoebic dysentery.** Amoebic dysentery is a serious parasitic disease. The protozoa *Entamoeba histolytica* has two forms—an active one that moves into the tissues and causes damage, and a cyst form. Victims of this amoeba can become infected anywhere in the world. If food and water with *Entamoeba histolytica* cysts are consumed, infection can occur. After entry into a host, the cyst becomes an active amoeba and lives in the large intestine, where it can cause deep ulcers in the intestinal wall. This results in the passage of blood in the stool.

Other species of amoebic parasites do not produce the severe symptoms of this one. All suspected amoebic infections should be treated promptly at the first symptoms. The diarrhea and dehydration that result from this infection are a serious problem for the victim.

Giardia lamblia—**giardia.** This is another protozoan that causes diarrhea. It enters the body when we drink infected water or eat food that contains the cyst form. This parasite has a tear-drop shape with several hairlike structures at the tail that propel it in fluid. The active forms are found in the victim's upper gastrointestinal tract. The cyst forms live in the lower small intestine and in the colon.

Trichomonas vaginalis—**trichomonas.** This is a protozoan that causes inflammation of the vagina and is considered a sexually transmitted disease. It is found in the urogenital tract of infected women and men. The parasite can cause a variety of annoying symptoms in women, but none in men. When we examine the parasite with a microscope, we find that it is the size of a large white blood cell with hairlike structures called flagellae. It can infect the urethra and may sometimes cause inflammation of the bladder (cystitis).

Testing for this organism requires a swab of vaginal fluid. A smear is made and then stained with a dye that will demonstrate all the characteristics of the parasite when viewed with a microscope. It can also be found by a cytotechnologist when examining a Pap smear. If it is not found in the smear, vaginal fluid can be cultured to grow the parasite.

An alternative to microscopic examination is serologic tests such as immunofluorescence and enzyme immunoassay to measure the antibody response of the host to the infection.

Toxoplasma gondii—**toxoplasmosis.** This parasite that lives in the intestine of the domestic cat causes toxoplasmosis, a serious illness. The complete life cycle of this parasite occurs only in a cat, and certain forms are excreted in cat feces. This may cause an infection in children playing in soil or near cat litter. Leafy vegetables contaminated with cat feces and not washed well before eating may also lead to toxoplasmosis in adults or children.

Toxoplasmosis can result in the enlargement of lymph nodes. In a long-standing infection, serious consequences can result, such as inflammation of heart muscle, liver tissue, or lung tissue.

A diagnosis is made by a clinical scientist or pathologist who recognizes these parasites in cytology slides, blood smears, or tissue sections. If the parasite is not found by these diagnostic methods, serologic testing by enzyme immunoassay can be used.

The *Plasmodium* genus of parasites—malaria. Malaria is a disease in warmer climates where there are swamps and damp conditions. Some mosquitoes of the genus *Anopheles* breed in these swamps and carry protozoans (one-celled parasites) that live in blood. The genus of these pathogens is *Plasmodium*, four species of which can cause human malaria—*P. falciparum*, *P. vivax*, *P. malariae, and P. ovale.* The one that can be fatal to man if not treated promptly is *Plasmodium falciparum.*

In all of these infections, the parasite completes its life cycle in human red blood cells. While developing in the mosquito and in man, the parasite changes into a number of different morphological forms. While inside a red blood cell, the parasite attaches to the wall of the cell, matures, and destroys the cell, releasing young forms. When many of these parasitic forms are in the bloodstream, causing red cell destruction, the patient develops an anemia.

Malaria caused by the bite of an *Anopheles* mosquito that carries *Plasmodium falciparum* results in a more severe illness than an infection by the other members of the genus. Symptoms of an established infection by this species are described briefly here. Periodically a patient experiences characteristic chills and a fever of up to 106° Fahrenheit. The white blood cell count is generally decreased, but there is an increase in monocytes. The liver and spleen may become enlarged. A microscopic examination of a biopsy of spleen tissue reveals the parasitic forms. When these events occur repeatedly, it leads to disability and chronic anemia. If treated promptly at the first symptoms, this infection can be eliminated.

Clinical diagnosis is made by finding malarial parasites in a special type of preparation. First, a thick circular smear of the patient's peripheral blood is made on a glass slide. This is an unusual type of smear because it is thick and composed of many layers of cells. The smear is dried and stained with the usual blood cell stains. The dyes provide a delicate coloration of the parasite as it resides within the red blood cell. This type of preparation allows us to examine each layer of the thick smear with a microscope so that many more parasites inside the red blood cells can be seen.

If the suspected parasite cannot be found by microscopic examination, diagnostic serological tests are performed to detect antibodies the patient has produced to fight the infection. When the parasite has been detected and identified, molecular biotechnology using polymerase chain reaction confirms the individual species of *Plasmodium* that is causing the illness.

Section 6. Parasites That Are Flatworms and Roundworms

A. Flatworms—Tapeworm

Some forms in the life cycle of flatworms are visible to the human eye. A group commonly called *tapeworms* is a well-known example. They are called tapeworms because when recovered from the stool of a victim, they resemble a long piece of tape. Upon close examination, however, the "tape" is sectioned into definite flat squares.

The resting stage of the worm is the cyst form. The cyst can infect us when we eat it in meat that is not cooked enough. While we are digesting the food, the cyst opens and releases the young tapeworm, which attaches to the intestinal wall and grows in length. The tapeworm is content there, consuming nutrients, which deprives the host of nourishment. Even though the victim of a tapeworm infection eats more food because of persistent hunger, a healthy diet alone is not the cure. Medicine is needed for full recovery.

Confirming the Presence of a Tapeworm

When the tapeworm is the suspected cause of this problem, a medication is prescribed. If it is effective, the tapeworm is recovered in a patient's stool. Diagnosis is made by identifying small sections of the worm, or the eggs using special preparations and microscopic examination.

The most common types of tapeworm found in contaminated meat are *Taenia solium* in pork, *Taenia saginata* in beef, and *Diphyllabothrium latum* in fish. All meat that we eat is inspected for these parasites. However, if a cyst or ovum should happen to be present in our food, it is killed when food is well cooked.

Another Species of Flatworm—The Fluke

This is a species of flatworm called trematodes that we cannot see without using a microscope. Trematodes have complex life cycles. The common name for them is *fluke*. Different species of trematodes can invade the intestine, the liver, the lung, or blood vessels. One of them is described here.

Clonorchis sinensis. A long-standing infection with this fluke means it resides in the bile passages of the liver. It can infect humans and some animals. There are intermediate forms called *cercaria*, which can be encysted under the scales of some fish.

Humans can become infected by eating these freshwater fish when they are raw or poorly cooked. There is a chance of acquiring it when eating pickled, smoked, or dried fish. If *Clonorchis sinensis* is present in meat products, it can be recognized by food inspectors and does not go to consumers. The adult fluke is visible to the human eye because it is 1 to 2.5 centimeters in length.

B. Roundworms

Enterobious vermicularis—**pinworm**. The roundworm is another classification of parasite that infects man. One is *Enterobious vermicularis*, the pinworm. A host is infected when swallowing the eggs of the parasite in contaminated food or when handling soil that has parasite eggs, then eating with unwashed hands. This may occur with children more than with adults.

The adult worm is very small, measuring an average of eight millimeters in length, and lives in the large intestine when we are infected. The female worm migrates to the anus of the victim to deposit her eggs. The tiny ova present in the host's anal area can be carried by the fingers to reinfect the victim. This happens usually with a child who is infected and does not wash properly after toilet use.

Confirming the Presence of a Pinworm

Diagnosis of a pinworm infection is made in an unusual way. A physician recovers the ova from the area surrounding the anus with a clear, two-sided adhesive tape attached to a tongue depressor. The tape is removed and attached to a glass slide, which is examined with a microscope by a microbiologist. The infecting ova can be seen clearly.

Trichinella spiralis—**trichinosis.** A common roundworm is *Trichinella spiralis*, which causes trichinosis. The origin of this parasite is an infected rat. Domestic pigs become infected when they eat rats. Then, the parasite forms cysts in the muscle tissue of pigs. When we eat undercooked pork, we can become infected.

After eating the infected pork, the larvae (an intermediate form of *Trichinella*) are released in the small intestine and develop into adult male and female worms. The average length is 2.5 millimeters. When the female releases larvae, they enter the host's blood circulatory system. The body defenses kill most of these migratory larvae. However, some of them reach skeletal muscle tissue, where they coil into a ball and form a microscopic cyst that survives for years.

In the infected person, the cysts can cause fever, muscle pain, edema around the eyes, and an increase in the number of eosinophil white blood cells when we examine the white blood cell differential count.

Confirming the Presence of *Trichinella*

For a diagnosis of trichinosis, a muscle biopsy is taken from the suspected cyst location. The fragment of muscle tissue is prepared by a histotechnologist and examined microscopically by a pathologist to locate the encysted form of the worm in the muscle fibers.

Numerous other parasites can cause diseases in man. This is only a brief description of some that could be encountered in modern living circumstances.

SECTION 7. VIRUSES AND DISEASES THEY CAUSE

A. Exactly What Is a Virus?

A virus is an infectious particle and not a cell. It is smaller than bacteria, but like bacteria it can cause disease in humans, animals, and plants. It is not able to move independently in the body, but it becomes attached to a cell in the moist tissues and blood. Then, it biochemically breaks down the cell membrane and enters.

Viruses contain nuclear material that is either deoxyribonucleic acid or ribonucleic acid, which direct the invaded body cell to produce another virus like the invader. In other words, the virus uses the proteins and enzymes of a body cell to produce more viruses like itself. All viruses are pathogens. They range in size from about twenty to three hundred nanometers. (A nanometer is one billionth of a meter.) When seen next to a bacterium, the difference in size is startling. (See the drawing on p. 188.)

B. How Do Viruses Invade Us?

The path of entry of most viruses is the respiratory tract by way of the nose, throat, and lungs or the gastrointestinal tract. They establish themselves and cause symptoms a long distance from where they entered the body. For example, an infecting virus can be found in cultures from the upper respiratory tract, while a rectal swab can also reveal the virus's presence. Later in the disease, an examination of cerebrospinal fluid can confirm the presence of the virus in the brain and spinal cord.

Viruses may also enter the body when we eat food contaminated with small amounts of fecal material. When food is prepared in unsanitary conditions, viruses and bacteria can enter the gastrointestinal tract.

Other Pathways of Infection

An injection by means of contaminated needles can be a source of viral infection. These microscopic invaders can also enter our bodies in blood transfusions or tissue transplants when their presence has not been detected by reliable clinical pretesting. Currently, there are governmental policies in place for extensive testing by donor collection centers and blood banks to ensure that blood products are free of viral and bacterial contamination.

C. How Do We Confirm Their Presence?

Testing Is Different for Viruses

The process of identifying an infecting virus begins with a swab taken by a physician from the throat, skin, nasal passages, or rectum, depending on the suspected source of the infection. The specimen is delivered to a clinical laboratory in a special collection tube that contains a "transport liquid" favorable for the survival of viruses.

In the virology laboratory, a suitable culture liquid is inoculated with a small amount of the specimen. Clinical scientists culture the virus, study its characteristics, and then identify it. When working in this clinical laboratory, a scientist wears protective gloves, a mask, and special clothing—all components of a biological safety cabinet.

Size comparisons of viruses with a bacterium

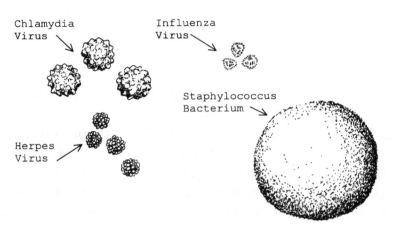

Culturing Viruses

Virus cultures comprise a liquid that contains a collection of living cells. Sometimes there is actual tissue floating in this special culture liquid. This unusual procedure is needed because viruses require conditions that closely resemble the body environment. They thrive in the culture liquid inside the tissue cells. The culture media include such things as baby chick tissue (from inside a fertilized egg) or liquid containing living monkey cells.

After the culture medium is inoculated with the specimen, the virus is allowed to grow in large test tubes made especially for this purpose. A large roller drum holds a number of these tubes in place while it slowly rotates, bathing all of the tissue cells. All of this takes place at an ideal temperature for growth. The tubes containing the cultures are examined daily.

When sufficient time has passed, the growth is examined

for virus-induced damage to the culture cells. In other words, the virus has entered the cells, causing their destruction. Each type of virus can be identified by the kind of cell damage that has occurred and by the type of cell that has been attacked.

D. Viruses and the Diseases They Cause

In the following section, different viruses and the diseases they cause are described briefly. You are probably familiar with most of the virus names.

Adenovirus—common cold. Members of the adenovirus family prefer to live on our mucous membranes. They live in the nasopharynx, which is the area behind the nasal cavity. Air entering here goes to the lungs. The openings to the eustachian tubes are located here with a connection to the middle ear where the virus can cause an infection. These viruses cause the common cold. This infection sometimes leads to pneumonia in young children and the elderly.

Cytomegalvirus (CMV). This virus can infect us in various ways. It may be acquired at birth or later in life by close contact with an infected person. When the infection is present, the virus is found in body fluids such as saliva, urine, breast milk, cervical secretions, blood, and semen. But both adults and children may be free of symptoms after infection has occurred.

Later, when symptoms do appear, the patient usually has fever and lethargy and may have abnormal lymphocytes, as seen in the white blood cell differential count. The usual diagnostic tests may be performed, such as a virus culture and serologic studies. Molecular biotechnology using polymerase chain reaction can also identify the virus.

Hepatitis. There are different types of hepatitis, and they are named A, B, C, D, or E, according to the type of virus that causes the infection. Viruses causing this illness belong to different families. Hepatitis A, B, and C will be discussed because they are the most common.

Hepatitis A is caused by the hepatovirus, which is composed of ribonucleic acid. We become infected when we consume contaminated food and water. Some shellfish may cause the infection when we eat them raw or when they are steamed to a temperature that does not kill the virus. This virus can be cultured in the virology clinical laboratory.

Hepatitis B is caused by a virus composed of deoxyribonucleic acid called the hepadnavirus. It can be transmitted in various ways, such as the handling of contaminated blood products; using contaminated needles in acupuncture, tattooing, or drug use; or eating food containing the virus. It can also be sexually transmitted.

This virus can cause an acute hepatitis and, in some cases, liver damage. Fortunately, an effective vaccine has been developed to prevent people from becoming infected. This is most useful to medical personnel who are in everyday contact with patients who may have the virus.

Hepatitis C is contracted most commonly through transfused blood products. Blood products are currently tested for hepatitis B and C viruses, so the risk of transmitting hepatitis from this source has been virtually eliminated. A second source of infection is contaminated needles used by intravenous drug users. The infection is less severe than hepatitis A and B, but there is a high incidence of it becoming a chronic condition.

Herpesvirus—herpes. This family of viruses includes herpes simplex, varicella-zoster virus, cytomegalovirus, and Epstein-Barr virus.

Infections caused by herpes simplex can be of two types. In general, type 1 invades the upper body and type 2 invades the genital tract. The typing is used to isolate these viruses in virology laboratory because type 1 herpes does not recur as often as type 2.

This virus causes a wide variety of infections, but those of the mouth and genital tract are the most common. In the oral cavity herpes simplex can cause a moderate gingivitis. After a patient recovers from the illness, the infection can recur at a later date because the virus remains dormant in the tissues. A herpes infection of the lip is known as a cold sore or fever blister. The outer part of the upper or lower lip is affected. Cold sores disappear in about a week.

In people with a weak immune system, herpes simplex can cause severe inflammation of the esophagus and of the bronchi. This may progress to generalized illness such as pneumonia and hepatitis.

When the virus attacks the genital area, it causes painful sores in and around the genital tract. Once acquired, it recurs periodically for many years and can be transmitted to sexual partners.

Other viruses in this family include the varicella-zoster virus, which causes chickenpox. It can live in a latent condition in the body for years and then reactivate, causing the disease "shingles."

Another member is the Epstein-Barr virus. It is discussed under "Infectious Mononucleosis (infectious mono)—(IM)."

Human immunodeficiency virus (HIV). HIV, distributed worldwide, is composed of ribonucleic acid. Its viral proteins are used as important diagnostic antigens when we test for its presence in blood or tissues. One of the antigens is a part of the virus called the envelope protein. It holds the key for the virus to enter body cells. For example, this antigen is attracted to the surface of certain T-lymphocytes and macrophages. Once attached, the virus reproduces itself and ultimately destroys the cell.

HIV enters the body most commonly by means of genital ulcers. Another route of entry is by using contaminated syringe needles for intravenous drug injections.

HIV is excreted in saliva, semen, and other body fluids. However, transmission of the infection has been documented only after exposure of a partner to blood or genital secretions.

Course of the Disease

The first signs of infection with HIV are fever combined with any of the following symptoms: lymph node enlargement, pharyngitis (a sore throat), or a diffuse rash. Antibodies to the virus develop months later. If the clinical laboratory is testing for viral antigens, there is a window of opportunity between when testing for the virus antigen is positive and antibody testing is negative. This is estimated to be about two months after infection has taken place.

The next phase of the disease is characterized by the presence of antibodies and low levels of circulating viral antigen. The virus changes genetically many times during this period as it survives in the patient's bloodstream. As a result of this trick, the host cannot produce specific antibodies to fight the infection. The host's immune system is eventually compromised because of this.

During this period, infections can occur by other viruses or by fungi, mycobacteria, other bacteria, and parasites. The clinical phase of an HIV infection is characterized by these repeated infections.

How Do We Confirm a Diagnosis?

HIV persists for these reasons, even though patients have developed some antibodies to it. Serologic tests to detect HIV antibodies or antigens are used because isolation and confirmation of the virus in cell culture is difficult. Other methods of testing for an HIV infection are discussed in the immunology/serology chapter.

Infectious Mononucleosis (infectious mono)—IM. This is a fairly common disease of the lymph system caused by the Epstein-Barr virus. The onset of the illness brings on a fever and sore throat with pus present. There are enlarged lymph nodes, especially in the neck, armpit, and groin. The differential white cell count reveals an increase in lymphocytes. Among them is a certain type of abnormal lymphocyte. A diagnosis of infectious mononucleosis can be made when these atypical lymphocytes are found in a blood smear and the physical symptoms are confirmed by a physician.

When the patient has recovered, a CBC is useful to show a decrease in these abnormal forms. There is a slow return to a normal white blood cell differential count during the next few months of the illness. Another test is the heterophile antibody test. Therapy is monitored for effectiveness with this test as well.

Papilloma viruses—human papilloma virus (HPV). Papilloma viruses include one hundred genotypes, thirty of which are spread through sexual contact. They enter the body by way of the skin, genital tract, or respiratory tract. An infection can cause common warts on the skin and laryngeal warts (on the voice box).

193

This group of viruses, which causes venereal warts, is one of the most common causes of sexually transmitted diseases (STDs) on a worldwide basis. Lesions appear on the skin or mucous surfaces of the genital areas. There is good evidence that this virus infection is a precursor to cancer of the cervix in women. When the typical viral infected cells are observed on the Pap smear, the patient's specimen can be sent for HPV typing to determine whether the infection is a high- or low-risk type.

Paramyxovirus—measles, mumps. This family causes serious illnesses such as measles and mumps. This varied group includes parainfluenza viruses, which cause laryngitis and bronchitis in children between two and six years of age. Infections occur all year, but peak in the fall and spring. Vaccines given to children at an early age have reduced the incidence of these infections in the United States.

Orthomyxoviruses—influenza. This group includes the influenza viruses A and B, which produce a wide variety of respiratory infections. These infections usually occur during the winter. Influenza (flu) begins with a headache, fever, chills, and a dry cough. Eventually, the symptoms are a high fever, muscle aches, and loss of appetite. Flu vaccines are provided for this virus infection in the late fall of each year.

Rabies. This is a rare infection in the United States. It is caused by a virus of the rhabdovirus group, which is distributed all over the world and can be present in wild animals in the United States. Rabies is caused by a virus entering our bodies through the bite of an infected dog, squirrel, bat, or other mammal. The virus is transmitted to the victim when the protective skin of the body is broken and blood vessels are exposed. Rabies in a human can be fatal if not attended to immediately after being bitten. A vaccine regimen administered soon after receiving a bite prevents the victim from having a severe form of the infection.

A necessary precaution is to have pets vaccinated regularly to prevent a rabies infection. Exceptional care should be taken when handling wild animals such as rabbits and squirrels because they could be infected.

Smallpox. This disease, caused by the variola virus, is a serious, contagious one that had been considered extinct in the United States. However, after the attacks of September 11, 2001, there is concern that the virus may be used for bioterrorism, so interest has been revived.

There are several forms of smallpox, but the most common one causes an extensive rash and high fever. Humans are the only natural hosts for variola, and it is not transmitted by insects or animals. Infection can spread quickly from person to person in saliva droplets when sneezing or speaking in proximity. When we are in contact with infected body fluid or contaminated objects, we can get it.

The virus can be transmitted to another person in the saliva of a patient in the first week of illness. The first symptoms are fever, headache, body aches, and sometimes vomiting.

When the disease is established, a characteristic rash appears on the face, arms, and legs. The patient is most contagious when this rash is present. It develops into flat, red lesions that fill with pus. Scabs form, then fall off within three to four weeks. The patient is contagious until all scabs have fallen off. The majority of people with smallpox infection recover.

West Nile virus (WNV). This is spread by the bite of an infected mosquito. People as well as horses, many types of birds, and other animals can become infected, but human victims of this disease are rare.

Most infected people will have no symptoms or mild ones. It cannot be spread from person to person or from animal to person. If there are dead birds in your vicinity, it is a good idea to report them to the authorities. It may mean that WNV is circulating between birds and mosquitoes in your area.

Some symptoms of the mild infection are loss of appetite, headache, muscle pain, fever, and nausea. These complaints last for three to six days. The more severe infection has some of the same symptoms and, in addition, weakness and gastrointestinal problems. Most people recover from this severe form of the disease.

Prompt Attention Provides Good Results

All of these infections are carefully considered by a physician when he sees a patient who has typical complaints. The physician performs a physical examination and makes a tentative diagnosis. A specimen is collected for the microbiology laboratory. Tests are performed to identify the virus. The immune response of the patient is measured in the immunology clinical laboratory.

Additional information can be obtained in Elmer W. Koneman, S. D. Allen, W. M. Janda, P. C. Schreckenberger, and W. C. Winn Jr., *Color Atlas and Textbook of Diagnostic Microbiology* (Philadelphia: J. B. Lippincott, 1997).

chapter 6

Immunology and Serology

I n this clinical laboratory, we measure the ability of the immune system to fight an infection. This is done by detecting the buildup of antibodies by a host during the period of infection. It may be caused by bacteria, fungi, a parasite, or a virus. The specimen studied is usually blood serum.

SECTION 1. A FEW FACTS ABOUT THE IMMUNE SYSTEM

Why Is It Important to Study Blood Serum?

The word *serology* means the study of serum. You know from your reading that serum is the clear, straw-colored liquid that remains in a test tube after blood has clotted. Serology testing has to do with investigating the products of our immune system because serum contains the immune proteins, or immunoglobulins.

Tests performed in serology laboratory measure the efficiency of our defense against proteins that are not ours. If a substance gets into our system that has not been encountered before, several things could happen. If it is a pathogenic organism, an infection results. If the foreign protein is not a pathogen, an allergy could result. In both instances, the immune system is involved.

In a broad sense, *immunity* means the body's resistance to different things in the environment, such as microorganisms of all kinds, foreign substances, and what we might refer to as poisonous substances or toxins. In some diseases, this resistance extends to our own living cells, resulting in, unfortunately, antibodies to our cells.

Antigens and Antibodies Not Involving Infection

Substances capable of stimulating the immune system are called antigens. We are all familiar with the blood groups, also called blood types. They arise from antigens on the surface of red blood cells present naturally from birth. They determine the blood group we belong to. Other types of antigens are in our tissues. These are important when we receive tissue and organ transplants.

As we delve further into this protective system, we find that when an immune system is exposed to an antigen that is not its own, the body responds. The result is the production of a specific antibody against the antigen. The word *specific* means that the antibody was produced by our immune system to react only with the antigen that caused its production.

Just a small part of our defense system reacts to an antigen at one time. As a result, we are capable of reacting to several different antigens when they are present in the body. Let us focus on a single antigen now. At the time of our first exposure, the immune system becomes sensitive to it, but we are not aware of this. After this encounter, the immune system is prepared to respond the second time it meets the antigen. On the second or third exposure, depending on the individual, a pronounced response occurs.

An example of this is an Rh negative mother whose immune system becomes sensitized to a fetus whose red blood cells are Rh positive. Sometimes there is fetal-maternal bleeding during the pregnancy, and the fetal blood cells enter the mother's circulation. More often, however, fetal cells get into the circulation of the mother at the time of birth. The first Rh positive baby may escape the result of antibody formation, but, in later pregnancies when a fetus is again Rh positive, more antibodies have been produced and are harmful to the fetus. These antibodies enter the blood circulation of the developing baby, where they destroy red blood cells. A transfusion of compatible blood is given to the newborn if an anemia has developed as a result of the destroyed red blood cells.

Antigens and Antibodies That Involve Infection

Different Kinds of Immunity

You are now aware that when antibodies are formed by the body after exposure to foreign substances, you are protected. There are two ways that antibodies protect us—active immunity and passive immunity.

Active Immunity

Active immunity results when you are exposed to an infectious agent or have contracted the disease it causes. In both of these instances, the immune system forms antibodies against the invading bacteria or virus.

Another way to create active immunity is by injecting a solution containing antigenic substances of the infecting microbe into the skin to stimulate antibody production. This liquid is called a vaccine, which is made up of suspensions of weakened or killed bacteria or viruses. Sometimes the vaccine is composed of bacterial or viral products that are no longer toxic, which can also act as antigens. The purpose of a vaccine is to stimulate the production of antibodies without a patient having clinical symptoms of the disease. This type of immunity lasts for years because we have produced the antibodies against it.

Passive Immunity

A second type is passive immunity, which occurs when a person is injected with ready-made antibodies. It is an artificial immunity because the injection we receive contains a high concentration of antibodies that we have not produced. This type of immunity provides immediate protection against a microorganism. The antibodies have usually been produced by an animal that has been actively immunized.

Passive immunity provides temporary, short-lived protection for as long as antibodies survive in the circulating blood. An example of this type of immunity is when a developing fetus receives antibodies from the mother's circulation. They are passed through the uterine blood vessels and the placenta. This explains why babies in their first few months of life have a natural immunity to some infections they are exposed to.

Immunoglobulins: The Real Antibodies

Where Do They Come From?

Antibodies are produced by lymphocytes of the immune system after we are exposed to an antigen. Antibodies are really lymphocyte-produced proteins. We can identify these proteins when we test serum for their presence. The scientific name for them is immunoglobulins (Igs). There are different kinds of immunoglobulins, and they are divided into five classes. We refer to each of them as IgG (gamma globulin), IgA (alpha), IgM (mu), IgD (delta), and IgE (epsilon). When we test a sample of patient's serum by electrophoresis, these fractions separate into distinct bands on the test medium. Then, a clinical scientist is able to determine the type of immunoglobulin and the amount present in a patient's serum.

Some Immune Complexes Can Be Harmful

Ordinarily, when an antigen and antibody combine in tissues or in blood, the combination is removed by phagocytic white cells and tissue macrophage cells. These specialized cells get rid of waste products in our blood and tissues. *Phagocytosis* means that certain cells are able to surround these wastes and destroy them biochemically. Normally, this function is not harmful and is considered a good defense against the invasion of foreign substances like bacteria or pollen. Sometimes, however, these immune complexes escape the phagocytes and persist in the blood. This is serious because they stick to blood vessel walls and cause inflammation. The immune complexes may be deposited in the tiny capillaries inside vital organs such as the kidneys, where they can cause damage.

This type of activity contributes to autoimmune diseases, in which the immune system reacts in a harmful way to our own cells. Some autoimmune diseases are discussed in the hematology chapter of this book.

SECTION 2. SEROLOGICAL TESTING PRINCIPLES AND SOME METHODS

The Basis for Serologic Tests

Testing procedures to detect and measure the activity of the immune system are complex. Most of these tests determine whether antibodies are present in a person who has been exposed to the antigenic protein of a bacteria or virus. When a test solution containing some form of the antigen is mixed with a patient's serum, a reaction occurs if antibodies are present. This reaction is called *agglutination. Precipitation* is a term also used to describe this reaction, but there is a slight difference between these terms. Agglutination describes the clumping or aggregation of particulate test antigens, while precipitation describes the aggregation of soluble test antigens. These reactions in a test system allow us to estimate the strength of a patient's response to the invader and at the same time identify it.

For example, a positive agglutination test when using an antigen of *N. gonorrhea*, lets us know that this bacteria is the infecting agent. The strength of the battle the patient's immune system is waging can be seen in the amount of agglutination that results from the combining of antigen and antibody. The reaction can be measured in several ways—on glass slides, in test tubes, or with special equipment. The following diagram shows agglutination and a negative reaction using glass slide and test tube methods.

Some Ways of Making Them Visible

These antigen/antibody complexes are not seen with the human eye. In order to judge the strength of the reactions, we make them visible. Several things can be done to make the immune combinations observable and measurable.

a) One of the first of these aids was the addition of latex particles to an antigen or an antibody. For example, in one procedure, antibodies to C-reactive protein are bound to tiny latex beads by the manufacturer. If C-reactive protein is present in the patient's specimen, it will bind with the antibody on the latex beads. This is easily seen.

b) Sometimes an automated instrument is used to count electronically the immune complexes in a liquid solution after they have been labeled with a dye.

c) Radioactive isotopes that do not give off dangerous levels of radioactivity can be used to tag the antigen or antibody. The amount of radioactivity detected by the combined particle is measured.

d) Dyes that give off a fluorescent glow in ultraviolet light when antigen and antibody combine make good labels.

e) Another means of measuring the combining of antigen

Slide and test tube agglutination

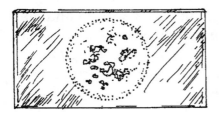

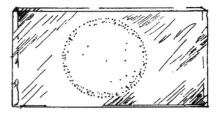

Positive Reaction
Slide

Negative Reaction
Slide

Positive Reaction
Test Tube

Negative Reaction
Test Tube

and antibody is to change them into colored products by means of an enzyme reaction. Instruments can be used to measure the resulting color.

206

f) Chemical luminescence is a current technology in which the chemicals used as reagents in the test give off light. They do not need ultraviolet light to become visible. The chemiluminescent labels are attached to an antigen or antibody. When there is a combination of the two, a flash is emitted and measured by a laboratory instrument. This method can be used to identify proteins like viruses and genomic nucleic acids.

Procedures of Interest

Flocculation Tests

These are based on the interaction of a soluble antigen with its antibody. When they combine, a fine, visible precipitate forms. Some tests for syphilis, the venereal disease, are based on flocculation. Two are the venereal disease research laboratory (VDRL) and the rapid plasma reagin (RPR) tests. When positive, these tests are confirmed by a fluorescent antibody test.

Precipitation Reactions

Some precipitation tests are performed in a semisolid gel called agarose. It is transparent and colorless and neither acid nor basic. The antigens can be bacteria or some bacterial parts. The antibodies are those produced by the patient.

In the test system, these two elements move toward each other on the agarose medium. When they react, they bind together to form a visible precipitate in the form of a band. The shape of the band and the density of the precipitate are important because they reveal the extent of the disorder. This precipitation reaction is used in what is called immunodiffusion tests. Diffusion refers to the movement of the antigen and antibody toward each other.

Fluorescent Antibody Tests—Immunofluorescence

A fluorescent dye used as a label for antigens or antibodies is called immunofluorescence. The dye that is added to the test system is fluorescent, which allows it to glow in the darkened microscope field. In this procedure, antigens suspected of being in a patient's tissue biopsy or in his or her cell preparation are used. The tissue or the cells are exposed to a solution of known antibodies that have been labeled with fluorescent dye.

There is a reverse to this procedure—the detection of unknown antibodies in a patient's serum. A known labeled antigen is added to the test system, and when antibodies are provided by the patient's serum, fluorescence occurs. Both of these procedures confirm the presence of disease and provide a diagnosis.

The ultraviolet light of the fluorescent microscope allows us to see the combination of antigen and antibody because one or the other has been tagged with a dye. Two of the dyes used for this test are rhodamine and fluorescein. The amount and intensity of the fluorescence is measured and reported.

All of these tests are useful indicators of a reaction taking place between the antigen and antibody in a test system. They represent complex testing procedures that measure the competency of our immune system after it is challenged.

Fluorescent antibody test

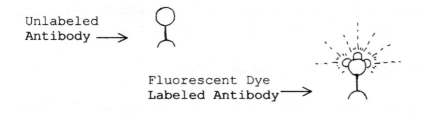

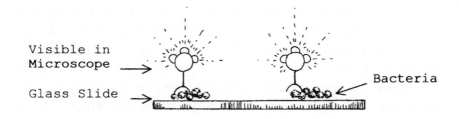

SECTION 3. PUTTING THE DISEASES AND TESTS TOGETHER

After reading this far, you know that one purpose of testing in a serology laboratory is to find antigens that belong to pathogens. Another is to find antibodies that have been produced by the host to fight these pathogens. In this section, various types of infections are described briefly. Test methods used to detect the pathogens are mentioned. At the end of the section, there is a quick reference of the tests used for diagnostic purposes. Some of the test methods make use of molecular biotechnology. This type of testing is replacing some of the traditional methods.

More information about diseases mentioned in this section can be found in the microbiology and hematology chapters. The disorders are in alphabetical order.

Antinuclear Antibody (ANA) Test

This tests for antibodies that act against the nuclei of one's own body cells. The victim of the antibody attack is called a target cell which can be in any tissue of the body and is destroyed by the antibody.

An antinuclear antibody reacts with DNA, which is in the cell nucleus. It is important to identify these antibodies and to find out how many there are. By testing we can find out which is the target tissue, and, with treatment, we try to minimize the destruction.

When an antinuclear antibody test is performed, the antigen-antibody combinations glow in the darkened field of a fluorescent microscope. This type of antibody is present in varying amounts in systemic rheumatic diseases such as systemic lupus erythematosus (SLE), discussed in the hematology chapter.

Anthrax Bacillus

For cases of suspected anthrax infection, laboratory testing is essential to the diagnosis. The first step is a dry mount of the specimen and a Gram stain to observe the morphology of the bacteria. The type of specimen will vary depending upon where the infection is located. (The microbiology chapter provides details of the infection.) Additional testing includes a bacterial culture of the patient's blood or spinal fluid. There may also be microscopic examination of infected tissue. A fluorescent antibody test also assists in identifying the bacteria. An important molecular biotechnology test is the polymerase chain reaction to find out whether the DNA of anthrax is present in the specimen. Serologic tests that will detect whether an individual has been exposed to this bacteria are currently being developed.

Autoimmune Diseases

These are disorders of the immune system that result in the formation of an immune complex that targets certain cells, causing them to die or lose their ability to function properly. Examples of this type of disorder are SLE, rheumatoid arthritis (RA), and Grave's disease of the thyroid. Diagnosis is made with the rheumatoid factor test and the ANA test and by identifying and measuring the quantity of each type of immunoglobulin present in the serum.

Some autoimmune disorders act differently with an unfortunate result. An example is autoimmune hemolytic anemia (AIHA), an attack on the patient's red blood cells. The cells are destroyed prematurely because of changes in the immune system, resulting in this unusual antibody activity. Testing is done to find the antibodies on the RBC surfaces.

Several diseases occasionally result in an AIHA, including chronic lymphocytic leukemia and some types of lymphoma. A thrombocytopenia (a decrease in the platelet population) may accompany a hemolytic anemia.

Beta-Hemolytic Streptococci—Strep Throat

This infection occurs by way of the respiratory tract when we are in close contact with infected individuals. The organisms are classified as Group A, a subgroup of the streptococcus family. The antigens of these pathogens are identified by using latex agglutination and immunoassay tests.

A useful way of detecting this dangerous member of Group A streptococci is to test for the toxin it produces when it infects us. When this is found, a clinical scientist can identify beta-hemolytic strep as the culprit. The toxin streptolysin O is released into the tissues during the infection and stimulates the production of antibodies called antistreptolysin. The test measures the patient's antistreptolysin response to the bacterial toxin. It is useful for confirming the presence of recent streptococcus infections.

Botulism—Food Poisoning

This is an infection caused by consuming the bacteria *Clostridium botulinum* in contaminated food. A preliminary diagnosis can be made in the microbiology laboratory by means of a dry mount and Gram stain. Confirmation of the clinical diagnosis of botulism food poisoning takes place in reference clinical laboratories such as the Centers for Disease Control and Prevention or the public health laboratories. The scientists in these laboratories test for the bacterial toxin in serum, feces, and the stomach contents of suspected victims.

C-Reactive Protein (CRP)—Rheumatoid Arthritis

This serological test detects a protein present in some chronic diseases. When present in human serum, it is a sensitive indicator of inflammation. The test is used to diagnose and determine the progress of rheumatoid arthritis, acute rheumatic fever, and advanced malignancy. Inflammation and tissue destruction from these disorders gives rise to C-reactive protein in the blood of these patients. Current research has found that C-reactive protein is a good predictor of cardiovascular disease (CVD) when combined with high levels of VLDLs and LDLs.

When a serological test is performed, CRP is the antigen and the corresponding antibody is attached to the surface of latex particles. Agglutination is seen when CRP is present.

Gonorrhea—STD

Neisseria gonorrhea is the causative agent for this sexually transmitted disease. Because the organism is very difficult to culture on laboratory growth media, we use unusual collection techniques to get a sample. For example, some of the secretion from the infected site is placed directly into media that contain nutritives for culturing it. This eliminates the use of a laboratory transport test tube. After carefully culturing the bacteria from the secretion, fluorescent antigen-antibody testing or enzyme immunoassay is used to determine the severity of the infection and the extent of the patient's response. Molecular biotechnology is also used in the form of DNA probes and polymerase chain reaction, which are described in the molecular biotechnology chapter.

Helicobacter pylori

This organism is suspected of being associated with duodenal ulcers and some forms of stomach cancer. The diagnosis of gastritis (inflammation of the stomach wall) and a possible *H. pylori* infection can be made when a physician examines the stomach wall by means of endoscopy. A simpler solution makes use of current blood tests for antibodies to *H. pylori* that are diagnostic for the infection.

Polymerase chain reaction can also identify the microbe. At-home testing includes a urea breath test, which, when positive, can identify *H. pylori*. These tests can also be used by physicians to monitor the infection after treatment has begun.

Hepatitis A

Serological tests detect hepatitis A antibodies when this infection is suspected. The enzyme immunoassay is one of the tests used to find out about a patient's immune response to the viral infection. If the infection is acute, the liver function test of alanine aminotransferase (ALT) is used to assess damage to the liver.

Hepatitis B (HBV)

An effective vaccine has been developed to prevent people who have been exposed to this virus from developing the disease. In some cases of hepatitis B infection, an antibody is produced that eliminates the virus from the system, and, as a result, the disease does not develop.

Other people, after recovering from the infection, continue

to circulate the viral antigens in their bodies. These individuals become carriers of the virus and can infect others.

The hepatitis B virus has surface antigens that are used when performing serological tests. Antigens in the core of the virus may also be used. Tests used to detect antigens are the enzyme immunoassay and polymerase chain reaction.

Hepatitis C

The laboratory diagnosis of hepatitis C by serological methods detects viral antigens or the antibodies a patient has produced. Molecular biotechnology methods of DNA and RNA analysis detect this virus.

Human Immunodeficiency Virus (HIV)

Diagnosis of an HIV infection is made by several methods, including antibody detection by enzyme immunoassay. This is used as a screening test for units of blood to be used for transfusion. It is also useful as a preliminary test to detect the infection when a person has been exposed to infected blood or body fluid. It is sensitive and specific for identifying the virus.

An RNA test using polymerase chain reaction has been developed to detect HIV infections. Positive results by any of these methods are confirmed by the Western blot test, in which the patient's serum reacts with different proteins of the virus. The test has many procedural steps and is highly complex.

Infectious Mononucleosis—Infectious Mono

This infection is caused by the Epstein-Barr virus. The serological test for infectious mononucleosis is a slide agglutination

215

test. The patient's serum is mixed with a special antigen preparation that has been attached to a test slide by the manufacturer. The reaction that takes place on the slide detects a special antibody called the heterophile antibody. The patient's immune system produces this when the infection is present, so a positive result means the patient has IM.

Lyme Disease

This is caused by the spirochete *Borrelia burgdorferi* and is usually carried by a hard-bodied tick. The serological tests used to confirm the presence of antibodies to *Borrelia burgdorferi* are fluorescent antibody tests and enzyme immunoassay. A positive result is confirmed by a Western blot test and a detailed patient history.

Meningitis

A bacterium that causes meningitis is *Neisseria meningitides*. Viruses can also cause meningitis. The bacterial infection can be detected by using a fluorescent antibody test. Different strains of the organism are determined by a test for the manner in which it metabolizes carbohydrates. Slide agglutination tests are also used to identify the bacteria. Other methods of identification are enzyme immunoassay and polymerase chain reaction.

Rabies

The diagnosis of a rabies infection is made by detecting the antigen of the causative virus in tissue from infected animals or from humans who have been bitten by rabid animals. A fluorescence test is an accurate and speedy way to make a diagnosis. There is also an enzyme immunoassay test for rabies infection.

Rheumatoid Arthritis

This is a disease in which inflammatory changes occur in the muscles, joints, and skeletal system. When it is a long-standing illness the lungs, heart, and blood vessels can be affected. A patient's serum may contain antibodies known as rheumatoid factor (RF). This means that antibodies have been produced against the protein globulin. If these RF antibodies are present, agglutination of latex particles that have been coated with globulin takes place. Enzyme immunoassay is also used to diagnose this disorder.

These antibodies are also found in the blood of patients who have systemic lupus erythematosus, tuberculosis, and bacterial endocarditis. The antinuclear antibody test is positive in some of these patients.

Salmonella—Diarrhea

These bacteria attack the gastrointestinal tract and cause typhoid fever and enteric (relating to the intestine) fever with diarrhea. The organisms are identified by means of agglutination or precipitation tests, which combine patient's serum and an antigen of the infecting species. Each species of this genus has its own antigenic structure.

When a culture of the pathogen is suggestive of salmonella, the reaction of a portion of the culture to differential biochemical reactions in test-kit form identifies the culprit. Additional methods for individual species of *Salmonella* include enzyme immunoassay and DNA testing.

Shigella and *Escherichia*—Diarrhea

These organisms attack the gastrointestinal tract. Testing to identify species of the two genera, *Shigella* and *Escherichia*, is similar to testing for *Salmonella*. Namely, the reactions of a portion of the bacterial culture to differential biochemical reactions in test-kit form are observed so that the invader can be identified.

Escherichia coli is a common bacterium that inhabits the intestinal tract but can become a pathogen. An infection's severity is determined by agglutination or precipitation tests that show an antigen/antibody reaction. The antigens used belong to the species of *Shigella* or *Escherichia* suspected of causing the infection.

Smallpox—Variola Virus

A vaccine for smallpox contains a virus called *vaccinia*, which protects us from the variola virus. When given within four days after a person is exposed to the virus, the vaccine allows the victim to have a less severe illness. Testing for this disease includes isolating the virus from a patient's specimen by culturing it. Serology tests for antigen and antibody detection are enzyme immunoassay and fluorescent antibody tests.

Syphilis

Serological tests detect the sexually transmitted disease syphilis. The pathogen that causes this disease is *Treponema pallidum*, a spirochete.

One method used to confirm the diagnosis of syphilis is the fluorescent treponemal antibody absorption test (FTA-ABS). A killed suspension of *T. pallidum* spirochetes is the antigen. The patient's serum contains the antibody. A globulin tagged with fluorescent dye is added to the test system. A fluorescent display indicates a positive result when seen with the microscope. Precipitation tests for syphilis were described in section 2 of this chapter.

Tetanus

This infection, caused by the bacteria *Clostridium tetani*, results when the bacterial spores enter a wound or laceration of the skin. The vaccine protects us even when we receive it immediately after a cut or puncture wound. A tetanus diagnosis is based on a physician's clinical and physical findings. A latex agglutination test measures the antibody response in a patient. There is also an enzyme immunoassay test for antibody detection.

Trichomonas vaginalis

This parasite can be found in a dye-stained smear of vaginal fluid when it is the cause of an infection. It can also be discovered by a cytotechnologist when examining a Pap smear. A serological test for the parasite is by enzyme immunoassay.

West Nile Virus

We can acquire this virus infection from a mosquito bite. West Nile virus is carried by birds. The diagnosis is confirmed with a serum enzyme immunoassay test. The polymerase chain reaction test to detect RNA of the virus is used on spinal fluid when the nervous system is involved.

The PCR is also used to test material from dead birds and mosquitoes. The results of these tests show us where a virus has been migrating in the bird and mosquito population.

A Quick Reference for Serological Tests

The following is a listing of some diagnostic methods used in detecting the diseases mentioned in the serology and microbiology chapters. Some tests are performed in reference laboratories. Your physician may not be able to request all of them from your local clinical laboratory. A reference laboratory can be found for these requests.

Enzyme Immunoassays

> *Borrelia burgdorferi*
> cytomegalovirus
> Epstein-Barr virus
> hepatitis A, B, D
> herpes simplex virus (HSV)
> HIV
> mumps
> *Mycobacterium tuberculosis*
> *Mycoplasma pneumoniae*
> rabies
> rubella virus
> syphilis
> toxoplasmosis
> *Trichomonas vaginalis*

Radioimmunoassay (radioactive labels)

diphtheria antibodies
hepatitis A antigens
lymphocyte typing
Pneumococcus (pneumonia) antibodies
human papilloma virus (HPV)

Fluorescent Dye Immunoassays

antinuclear antibody
Chlamydia trachomatis
Entamoeba histolytica
Fasciola parasite
Giardia lamblia
Hemophilus influenzae
herpes simplex virus
Legionella pneumophilia
Rickettsia
rubella virus
staphylococcus
Streptococcus pneumoniae

Latex Agglutination Tests

Candida infections
Clostridium tetani
Coccidioides immitis
measles
Neisseria gonorrheae
Streptococcus pneumoniae

The immunological test procedures mentioned in this section are complex. The reagents for testing are biochemically and biologically standardized and expensive. New methodologies continue to be introduced by researchers throughout the world. Testing involves many steps that require experienced clinical scientists to perform. Many tests are done in large reference laboratories. Strict quality-control measures ensure reliable results. These immunological reactions are useful to physicians in discovering the cause of infections and disease in patients, making it posible for timely treatment and full recovery.

Additional information can be obtained in Mary Louise Turgeon, EdD, MT (ASCP), CLS (NCA), *Immunology and Serology in Laboratory Medicine* (St. Louis, MO: C. V. Mosby, 1996).

chapter 7

The Donor Collection Center and Blood Bank Laboratory

SECTION 1. INTRODUCTION

The Blood Bank Laboratory and Donor Collection Center are places in which identification of blood and tissue antigens and antibodies takes place. The basic concept of serological testing—that of combining an antigen and its specific antibody, resulting in agglutination—is used. The tests performed in this section of the clinical laboratory ensure us that the patient will have no adverse reaction upon receiving a donor's blood. This applies to tissue typing, where compatibility of donor and recipient is also needed.

SECTION 2. THE PRELIMINARIES

A purpose of finding out blood types is to provide a blood transfusion for someone who needs blood or blood components. It follows that the blood type of both the donor and the recipient must be determined. When a transfusion is needed, a donor must have the same type as the recipient. A sample of blood from a donor of the same blood type is chosen and tested with a sample of the patient's blood to find out whether they are compatible. This procedure is called the compatibility test. A traditional term for it is a cross-match for a transfusion. This testing matches the donor and recipient as closely as possible so that no reaction takes place when the transfusion is administered.

Donor Collection Centers

Most blood in the United States is collected by the American Red Cross or a community blood center. A few hospitals also collect enough blood to meet their transfusion needs. Before drawing blood, the donors are screened for past and present illnesses.

In one of these centers, the clinical laboratory scientist receives samples from all the collected units to test for infections and for antigens present on red blood cell surfaces. There are many antigens, but the most important ones when a transfusion is needed we commonly call the blood type. These antigens are accompanied by antibodies present in serum. As you may suspect, these are not the same type. The compatibility test assures us that the best match between donor and recipient is made. These procedures will be discussed in more detail.

SECTION 3. BLOOD GROUPING

Discovery of the Blood Group Antigens

Karl Landsteiner is the scientist who discovered the significant ABO blood group antigens in 1901 and determined the way

224

we inherit them. Scientists have since found that red cell surfaces have over six hundred antigens.

Landsteiner and his colleagues concluded from their studies that there are four distinct blood types, which belong to the ABO blood group system. Only two antigens, namely, A and B, are used to demonstrate the four blood types. Individuals who have the A antigen belong to group A, and those with the B antigen belong to group B. If both A and B are present, the person's blood group is AB. If neither antigen is present, then the individual is of group O.

Now things become more complicated. It was further observed that people who have A and B antigens do not have antibodies to A or B in their serum. These antibodies are called anti-A and anti-B. Because the same antigen and antibody are not simultaneously present in a person's bloodstream, type A people have the A antigen on their red cells and anti-B in their serum. Type B people have the B antigen on their red cells and anti-A in their serum. Type AB individuals have both A and B antigens on their red blood cells and neither antibody in their serum.

Type O people have neither A nor B antigens on their red cells and have both anti-A and anti-B antibodies in their serum. Type O people are considered universal donors who can donate blood to any other group. The lack of A and B antigens on their red blood cells ensures that no reaction will occur with anti-A or anti-B antibodies present in a recipient's serum. It is considered safe to use this blood to transfuse a patient of any blood type in emergency situations when blood is needed immediately. Blood used for emergency situations is usually type O and Rh negative. Rh antigens are discussed later in this chapter.

A diagram of the ABO system with the accompanying antibodies is shown here.

Classification of the ABO Blood Groups		
antigen on red cells	antibodies in serum	blood group
A	anti-B	A
B	anti-A	B
neither A nor B	anti-A & anti-B	O
A and B	neither anti-A nor anti-B	AB

Tests Performed in a Blood Bank Laboratory— Blood Type Testing

When this test is performed, some of the patient's red blood cells are combined with known commercial serum containing anti-A and anti-B antibodies. The goal is to identify the matching antigens on the red blood cell surface. The test can be done on a glass slide or in test tubes. After mixing the patient's cells with this commercial test serum, we look for an agglutination reaction to reveal the blood group. The same procedure is followed with donor blood. This test is called forward grouping for blood type.

The accuracy of this test is checked by a process of reverse grouping. Here we identify the blood group antibody present in the patient's serum by combining suspensions of known group A and group B red cells with the patient's serum. Signs of agglutination are looked for. Results of this test confirm the results of the forward grouping.

These tests are also performed on the donor's blood.

SECTION 4. HOW BLOOD GROUPS ARE INHERITED

You now know that these blood group antigens are present on the outer membrane of a red blood cell. They are inherited just like our other physical and biochemical traits. When fertilization of an ovum occurs, one gene for a characteristic such as the blood type is transmitted to the offspring from each parent.

The A and B blood group genes are co-dominant, which means that both gene characteristics are expressed. If group A gene and group B gene are inherited, both antigens are present and expressed. A person with this genotype belongs to the blood group AB.

A simple diagram demonstrates some patterns of heredity with parents of different blood groups.

Possible Offspring of Group A and Group AB Parents

Blood group of mother = AA
Blood group of father = AB

	A	A
A	AA [type A]	AA [type A]
B	AB [type AB]	AB [type AB]

These parents have a 50 percent chance of having a child with type A blood and an equal chance of having a type AB child.

227

SECTION 5. THE RH ANTIGEN

Grouping

The Rhesus (or Rh) blood group system is important and places second to the ABO system only. *Rh* is derived from the first two letters of Rhesus, a type of monkey. The history of this is interesting. It was found that when blood of a Rhesus monkey was injected into rabbits, the antibody that rabbits produced agglutinated red blood cells of approximately 85 percent of humans. Serum containing antibodies to the Rh factor—the unknown factor in the Rhesus monkey's blood—had been produced by the rabbit. The antigen involved in this test was named *D*, commonly called *big D*.

When this Rh D test serum is used with human red cells, a person's red cells containing the corresponding Rh D antigen become agglutinated. This person is considered Rh positive. When there is no agglutination, people lack the Rh D antigen and are considered Rh negative. Scientists have concluded from their research that 15 percent of humans are Rh negative.

The Rh system is complicated and is not dealt with fully in this book. Briefly, there are five different Rh antigens that clinical scientists can test for, namely, D, C, E, c, e. The capital letters indicate dominant (expressed) traits, and lowercase letters mean the trait is recessive. A recessive trait is expressed only when there is one recessive gene from the mother and one from the father. In a sense, the trait is usually hidden by the dominant gene. You will notice that there is no small *d* antigen.

There are combinations of these antigens on the red cells of every person. When testing is performed to determine the Rh type of a person, the presence of big D in the combination of antigens always indicates that the person is Rh positive. When D is not present in the test results, the individual is considered Rh negative. This is because D is the strongest of the five Rh antigens, and it can cause problems when an Rh negative person receives it in transfusion. It is the most frequent cause of hemolytic disease of the newborn (HDN); therefore, it is considered the most significant one when testing for Rh.

How Are Rh Antibodies Different from ABO Antibodies?

Antibodies to the ABO blood group occur naturally in the body, but antibodies to Rh are the result of a type of immunization reaction. In other words, the individual has made antibodies against an Rh antigen that was present in her blood at some time in the past. This could have resulted from a pregnancy in which the mother and fetus were of different Rh types, setting up an immune reaction in the mother. Another cause might have been a blood transfusion in which the donor was a different Rh type than the recipient. The resulting mild transfusion reaction might not have been noticed.

How Does the Rh Factor Complicate Pregnancies?

An Rh negative mother who gives birth to an Rh positive baby is exposed to Rh D antigens on the baby's red cells. The Rh D antigens present on fetal red cells cause the mother to develop antibodies because Rh D antigens are not present on her own red cells. These Rh positive antibodies enter the fetal circulation by way of the placenta, destroy red cells, and cause an anemia in the newborn infant.

This unfortunate result usually does not occur in the first

pregnancy, but the mother's immune system has been sensitized. In a second or third pregnancy, hemolytic disease of the newborn (HDN) could occur, giving an Rh D positive infant a serious anemia.

To minimize the damage to the infant, Rh immune globulin is given to the mother by injection. This minimizes the production of antibodies against the Rh D antigen of the fetus. Fortunately, hemolytic disease of the newborn is a rare occurrence.

Section 6. Compatibility Testing

The compatibility test proves that there is a match between patient and donor of ABO antigens and antibodies.

When a transfusion is to be given, this test is performed. It consists of mixing red blood cells belonging to a donor with the serum of a patient who will receive the unit of blood.

If no agglutination is present after examining the test tube visually, the blood unit is compatible with the patient's blood. But if agglutination is present, a search for an explanation is undertaken. The patient is not transfused with the donor unit, and the testing is repeated with a new donor unit.

More Tests for Antibody Identification

The ABO antibodies must be thought of as clinically significant. For example, if a mismatch should occur, A or B antibodies of the patient combine with the matching antigen on the red cell of the donor, causing rapid destruction of the donor's red cells. The transfusion is of little use for the patient.

For this reason, other antibodies must be identified.

Granted, we have tested for the main ones necessary for major compatibility, but we need to know whether others are present that may destroy transfused red cells. To find out about those that may be present, a screening test is performed. This consists of a panel of red blood cells with some important antigens that have been identified. Manufacturers of diagnostics have developed these reagents.

The patient's serum is tested for unexpected antibodies that may react with one or more of these panel cells. If the patient is found to have any of these, the donor unit is tested to be certain that donor red cells do not carry the matching antigen.

SECTION 7. THE AUTOLOGOUS TRANSFUSION

In hospital blood banks, it may be necessary to have compatible blood on hand when an individual is scheduled for surgery. But there is an alternative to receiving compatible blood from an unknown donor. A surgical patient may be able to store her or his own blood for a transfusion so that it is available if needed. This procedure is known as an autologous transfusion, in which a patient's blood is drawn several days to weeks prior to a scheduled surgery. Sometimes the autologous transfusion is allowed when a patient has an antibody to an antigen present on the red blood cells of most donors. The patient's own blood is valuable in this case. This blood can be stored until needed, but only for twenty-one to thirty-five days.

SECTION 8. DONOR INFORMATION AND BLOOD COMPONENTS

Donor Screening

The selection of blood donors must be done with great care. A prospective donor must be carefully screened and the donated blood tested. Donor screening includes a detailed medical history, a mini–physical examination, and a number of clinical tests.

Clinical Laboratory Testing

According to federal regulations, the donor sample must be tested for ABO blood type, the Rh antigen, and infectious agents such as the hepatitis B virus (core and surface antigen), HIV 1 and 2, hepatitis C, human T-cell lymphotropic virus (HTLV-I/II), and syphilis.

The American Association of Blood Banks (AABB) requires that tests for all types of known antibodies to red cell antigens be performed on samples from donors who have a history of prior transfusions or pregnancies. This assures the recipient that no known antibodies will cause a reaction. Since it is not practical to try to identify only those donors, these tests are performed on all donated units.

The federal Food and Drug Administration has approved tests for the human immunodeficiency virus (HIV) in donor blood. The current tests detect an antigen of the virus before there is a measurable buildup of antibodies. This is an advantage because the actual viral antigen can be detected early. Molecular testing for HIV using polymerase chain reaction is a new technique being used.

Preserving the Blood Unit after Collection

Blood banks in the United States preserve blood units to provide viable and functional blood components for patients needing transfusions. A blood bank aims to maintain red blood cell viability during refrigeration storage. The biochemical reactions of red blood cells are maintained best when the anticoagulants used in blood units are the preservatives citrate-phosphate-dextrose (CPD) or acid-citrate-dextrose (ACD).

Apheresis: A Means of Separating Blood

When a particular component of blood is needed, a special type of process called apheresis is performed. Apheresis is a Greek work meaning "to separate." This is most commonly performed to collect platelets. The procedure is performed in the American Red Cross centers and donor collection centers for blood testing and processing.

In this procedure, blood is removed from a donor and reagents are added to prevent coagulation. The blood is transferred directly to the apheresis instrument, where it is separated into specific components. After the separation, any one of them can be used for patient needs. These valuable machines need regular maintenance. Disposable software such as sterile bags, tubing, and collection chambers are required when performing apheresis routinely.

Obtaining these components is equally as important as preserving them in the best possible condition.

Component Therapy

In almost all situations, the components from apheresis are used instead of whole blood transfusions. This makes sense because by giving patients only the component they need— such as red blood cells, platelets, or coagulation factors—the other components can be used to treat more patients. As a result, several people can benefit from a single donation.

Types of Component Therapy

Red Blood Cells

There are different forms of red blood cell components, such as those used for anemias, for immune deficiencies, or for reducing febrile reactions that may occur in a patient.

Plasma

Several varieties of plasma components are also used. One is fresh frozen plasma or plasma frozen within twenty-four hours after collection, which may be administered to increase the level of a clotting factor in patients who have a deficiency in one of them.

Platelets

Pooled platelet components are used for bleeding problems due to a low platelet count or a functional abnormality of the platelets. Platelet components that have a low number of white blood cells are also available to reduce patient febrile reactions.

White Blood Cells

White blood cells, mainly granulocytes, are given to a patient with an infection that does not respond to antibiotics.

More information can be found in Denise M. Harmening, *Modern Blood Banking and Transfusion Practices* (Philadelphia: F. A. Davis, 1994); American Association of Blood Banks, American Blood Centers, and American Red Cross, *Circular of Information for the Use of Human Blood and Blood Components*, ARC 1751 (July 2002).

chapter 8

Urinalysis

SECTION 1. INTRODUCTION—
A COMMON BUT IMPORTANT TEST

The routine urinalysis test is of prime importance in assessing kidney function and valuable in finding out about the general health of an individual. The test is inexpensive and provides information for detecting kidney or urinary tract diseases.

There are two parts to the urinalysis test. The first part involves an examination of the physical and chemical characteristics of a urine specimen. The second part is a microscopic examination, which requires expertise and is time consuming. Either of these parts can be automated in today's urinalysis laboratory.

SECTION 2. THE RENAL SYSTEM

Vital Kidney Functions

The kidney filters our blood, reabsorbs some important elements, and excretes others as urine. The two kidneys—one on either side of the spine above the waist—can select and retain essential substances needed for normal body function. After blood has been filtered through the kidneys, the wastes that we do not need are excreted in the urine. Some of these are the products of body metabolism, and others are vitamins and minerals we have consumed in excess.

Kidneys also maintain the water balance in our tissues by working with the lungs to achieve water and electrolyte equilibrium in the body. In biochemistry language, this is referred to as acid-base balance. You recall the electrolytes that we discussed in the clinical chemistry chapter. They play an important role in our normal biochemistry. The importance of this is obvious when we consider that the composition of blood varies with different quantities of water, carbohydrates, fats, minerals, and proteins consumed.

Other factors should be considered when we talk about a true value for the electrolytes. One is the amount of physical activity we take part in because this uses up the blood nutrients and water. Also important is the purity of the air we breathe because the lungs help keep that electrolyte balance. Some water is lost when urine is excreted. This amounts to approximately one to two liters every twenty-four hours. It is clear that many factors must be investigated when assessing kidney health.

SECTION 3. THE DOCTOR EVALUATES TEST RESULTS

A physician uses several factors when evaluating the test results of a urinalysis. Again, the physical condition of a patient at the time the sample was obtained is important. For example, there may have been prolonged muscular activity or a period of fasting. There are unusual dietary habits to find out about in this day of "fad diets" and diet pills of all sorts.

Test results are affected if a patient has an alcohol or a drug addiction. The use of tobacco should also be considered. These things temporarily affect the urinalysis test results, so when they exist, they should be revealed to a physician.

SECTION 4. COLLECTING THE SPECIMEN

The Importance of Proper Specimen Collection

An accurate urinalysis test depends on a representative sample of daily urine output for an individual. Usually, a satisfactory urine sample is obtained by collecting it in the morning before any food or liquid is taken.

When certain products of body metabolism are measured in the urine, a large sample is needed. For example, a clinical scientist may ask for a urine sample that a patient collects over a twenty-four-hour period. In this instance, a person is given a large container and specific instructions on how to collect and preserve the specimen. A sample of this size represents the excretion of both kidneys over an extended period of time, allowing very small quantities of urine components to be measured. Examples of these products are cortisol or creatinine. A comparison of the amount of these substances present in both blood and urine is important when certain diseases are investigated.

The Timing of Specimen Collection and Testing

We all know the importance of using the container provided by the clinical laboratory to collect a specimen. Directions for collection should be followed closely. Ideally, the specimen is examined within one hour of the patient providing a sample. The first morning specimen is best for routine examination because it is a fairly concentrated sample and offers the best chance of recovering abnormal elements. These elements may be fragile and disappear if the testing is delayed too long. For reliable test results, all these factors are important quality-control measures that must be considered before the specimen arrives at the clinical laboratory.

In the Clinical Laboratory

Having reached the testing destination, there are additional considerations. If a urine specimen cannot be examined within one hour of being excreted by the patient, it is placed in the laboratory refrigerator until the testing process begins. Delayed testing jeopardizes the survival of red blood cells, white blood cells, and other cellular and crystalline structures suspended in urine. Also, bacteria may increase in number.

Extended delays cause deterioration, which makes some elements unrecognizable. Sometimes, they may actually disappear. Their presence in urine may indicate early kidney or bladder disease, so their preservation is vital. The presence of these elements is essential information for the physician in making an accurate diagnosis.

240

SECTION 5. THE TEST PROCEDURES AND THEIR MEANING

The urinalysis test begins with a clinical scientist or technician assessing the appearance of a specimen for color and clarity. After this is noted, tests are performed on the sample to determine the specific gravity, the presence of various proteins, glucose, ketone bodies, red blood cells, white blood cells, and different bile products. The urine pH, which provides a measure of acidity or alkalinity, is also determined.

For some of these determinations, a "dipstick" is used. This is a wandlike plastic strip approximately four inches long with small, colored test pads along one surface that have reagents for each test. These tests are qualitative in nature. This means that their presence is detected and roughly measured.

The Early Testing

After the appearance and clarity of a urine specimen is noted, the testing begins by using the described reagent strip. These strips represent multiple complex chemical reactions. In the test, a color reaction for an analyte may be different from the original color. The change in color demonstrates a variation from the normal amount of a substance, for example, glucose, proteins, or nitrites.

This color change of different parts of the strip allows a clinical scientist to quantitate roughly the analyte. If there is a strong positive reaction for one analyte, it is measured again by means of a specific test solely for that substance.

More about Dipsticks

The dipstick method for chemical analysis of urine provides a simple, rapid means of performing nine medically significant tests. The tests include: pH, protein, glucose, ketones, blood, bile products, nitrite, specific gravity, and an estimation of leukocytes.

The possibility of human error in reading color changes on the dipstick for the different analytes can be avoided by using semiautomated instruments. After the reagent strip has been used in a urinalysis test, it is inserted into this instrument, which automatically compares the color reflected from each segment of the strip to the color coming from known concentrations of each substance. This process provides a measurement of each test substance. The test result is then displayed or printed out as concentration units of the substance.

The Microscopic Part of the Test

The final part of urinalysis is a microscopic examination of urine sediment. The sediment is obtained after centrifuging a measured amount of urine in a special test tube at a specified speed and length of time. The formed elements (sediment) of the specimen collect at the bottom of the tube. After the liquid has been removed, a small portion of the sediment is placed on a glass slide, covered with a coverglass, and examined microscopically. The elements searched for in a urine sediment are described later in this chapter.

Individual Tests and Their Meaning

The normal pH of urine may range from 4.6 to 8.0, but, in good health, it is slightly acidic, at 6 to 7. Several things can be discovered when the pH is outside the reference range, such as electrolyte disorders. When there is an alkaline urine, with a pH of around 8, stones (calculi) can form in the microscopic tubules of the kidneys. So the high pH gives the physician a possible cause for the pain a patient has in the area of the kidneys.

The urine pH also helps clinical scientists to identify different types of crystals that may be found in urine sediment. Some crystals form only in acidic urine, while others prefer an alkaline environment. Crystal identification is important when a physician treats urinary tract infections.

Testing for Urine Specific Gravity

The specific gravity of urine is the ratio of the weight of a volume of urine to the weight of the same volume of distilled water when both are at a constant temperature. In other words, specific gravity estimates the concentration of dissolved material in urine. The substances that contribute to the specific gravity of urine in healthy people are urea, sodiuim chloride, sulfates, and phosphates. The reference range for specific gravity is 1.003 to 1.035.

This test is used to check out kidney function by giving us a measure of their concentrating and diluting ability. This is an important function, as kidneys maintain a balance of fluids in the body.

The specific gravity is low if a patient retains water. If the microscopic kidney tubules are damaged, the ability to concentrate urine is one of the first functions lost. Therefore, when kidneys no longer have the ability to do this, the specific gravity is low. As you can guess, when a patient is dehydrated, the specific gravity of urine is high because a lack of fluid makes the dissolved substances more concentrated.

This is all good information for the physician in assessing kidney function.

Protein in Urine

Increased amounts of protein in urine can be an important indicator of renal problems. If kidneys are functioning normally, only a small amount of protein escapes the filtration process and appears in urine. An increase in proteins usually occurs if there is damage to the microscopic kidney tubules.

The glomerulus is a microscopic unit of kidney tissue that filters blood. It has been estimated that there are several million glomeruli in each kidney. Damage to the glomeruli also causes albumin and other proteins to be excreted in excess.

What Do These Protein Values Mean?

The presence of detectable levels of a protein, such as albumin, in urine may indicate temporary or chronic kidney failure. Although albumin is present in high concentration in plasma, the content of this protein in urine is normally low.

When a urine sediment is examined with a microscope, the presence of albumin is suspected if renal casts are seen. Casts are composed of certain proteins and various other elements such as white blood cells, red blood cells, and epithelial cells. Renal casts are discussed later in this chapter.

Some diseases in which protein in the urine reaches high levels of the reference range are glomerulonephritis (an inflammatory condition of the kidneys), systemic lupus erythematosus (an autoimmune disorder that can involve the kidneys and blood vessels), and diabetes mellitus. Minor elevations of protein may also occur when a person has hypertension (high blood pressure) and during a pregnancy.

Important Indicators

Some of the important proteins that must be detected when they show up in a urinalysis are glycoprotein, Tamm-Horsfall mucoprotein, and Bence-Jones protein. You can find some of these listed on your clinical laboratory report. When the dipstick test shows an increase in proteins, then individual test procedures must be done to find out which protein level is abnormally high. Each protein's presence can signal possible early disease that can be reversed.

Preliminary Testing for Glucose

The detection of glucose in the urine is an important test for discovering early diabetes. Glucosuria (sugar in the urine) occurs when the blood glucose level is more than 180 to 200 milligrams in each deciliter of serum. A small amount of sugar may be present in a normal specimen, but the fasting level of urine glucose in adults is "none to very low" amounts. So when we find a detectable amount in a fasting sample with the dipstick test, it must be verified by testing for glucose in the blood serum. In this way, a patient obtains a timely detection of diabetes.

Testing for Ketones

Ketones are intermediate products of fat metabolism. Under normal conditions, they do not appear in urine because fat that we digest is eventually broken down into carbon dioxide and water by our body chemistry. However, in disorders such as diabetes mellitus, or when we are on starvation diets, body fat supplies energy instead of the usual carbohydrates. This increased use of fat for energy results in the appearance of ketone bodies in the urine. So when ketone bodies are found in a specimen, the cause must be investigated.

Testing for Blood

Blood may be present in urine as intact red blood cells. This condition is called hematuria. The presence of a moderate amount of blood cells gives urine a visibly pink color. But if urine contains only a small number of red blood cells, it will appear slightly cloudy.

Hematuria may be a clinical finding when calculi are present in the tiny kidney tubules or in a collection area called the kidney pelvis. Calculi can cause severe pain.

Other kidney disorders result in red blood cells in urine. These occasions should be investigated because even a small amount of blood is clinically significant for a patient.

The Presence of Blood in a Different Form

Hemoglobinuria (hemoglobin in the urine) results in a clear red urine specimen. It means that red blood cells have burst, releasing free hemoglobin. This happens in serious conditions such as hemolytic anemias, severe burns over large areas of the body, or as a result of a transfusion reaction. A clear red urine specimen received in the clinical laboratory is quickly investigated.

Bilirubin or Bile

When an elevated bilirubin value is detected in urine, it may be the first sign of a liver disorder. This could provide us with the early detection of hepatitis, cirrhosis, cholecystitis (inflammation of the gallbladder), or a carcinoma. Therefore, the cause of elevated values is investigated with further testing. The story of bilirubin formation and transport was told in the clinical chemistry chapter.

Nitrite

The presence of nitrites in urine is a sign of urinary tract infection. A dipstick is useful to detect nitrites when the infection is not obvious to a patient or physician. A positive finding indicates that a culture of the urine specimen should be obtained.

Positive nitrite values may indicate cystitis (an infection of the urinary bladder) or some type of kidney disorder. In case of cystitis, after the invading bacteria are identified by culture or by serological tests, an effective antibiotic is found and treatment is started. The simple dipstick test is also useful when a physician wants to assess the effectiveness of antibiotic therapy he has provided.

SECTION 6. FINDINGS IN A MICROSCOPIC EXAMINATION

The final part of a urinalysis test is the microscopic examination of urine sediment. This type of specimen is obtained after spinning a portion of the urine in a centrifuge tube at a specified speed and length of time. A small button of cells and other elements collect at the bottom of the tube. This is the sediment. A portion of it is transferred to a glass slide and covered with a small coverglass. Using a microscope and a magnification of one hundred times, and then four hundred times, a clinical scientist can see different types of structures.

Some of them are red blood cells or white blood cells; others are epithelial (surface) cells from different parts of the urinary tract. Chemical crystals of various types and renal casts may be present. These must be identified and reported.

The Microscopic Findings

In reading this book, you have encountered information about red and white blood cells. These elements are found in the urine sediment in certain illnesses. In normal urine, one or two red blood cells are found in a microscopic field. More than three is considered over the limit. The presence of increased numbers may indicate kidney disease. In other instances, there may be an inflammation of the kidneys associated with drug reactions, stones in the tiny renal tubules, a tumor present in the urinary system, or an infection.

A few white blood cells may also be found upon microscopic examination of normal urine. More than a few indicates the presence of infection or inflammation of the urinary tract.

Cast

Casts are cylinders of protein and mucous that form inside of the microscopic filtering and collecting tubules of the kidneys. When certain types of casts are found, it is a sign to the clinical scientist that the kidneys may be malfunctioning.

Certain characteristics of urine favor cast formation, including a concentrated rather than dilute urine, and the presence of an increased amount of protein. To explain further, when urine is flowing through the excretory system at a slower-than-normal rate because of these factors, cast formation is enhanced.

Crystal Formation

Crystals form in the urine and are seen upon microscopic examination when there is a change in pH, temperature, or the concentration of a substance. Cystine crystals are associated with cystine calculi. Leucine and tyrosine crystals are seen in liver disease. Sulfonamide crystals can be present as a result of drug therapy. Other crystals can be present and identified.

Usually, no cellular casts are seen in a normal urine sediment, but there may be an occasional one. When a cast contains red blood cells, the glomeruli have been damaged by a kidney disorder. White blood cell casts contain mainly neutrophils, and their presence indicates a kidney infection or inflammation.

The result of a microscopic examination of urine sediment is reported as the average number of cells, crystals, casts, and so forth found in ten or more microscopic fields of view.

Some elements seen in urine sediment

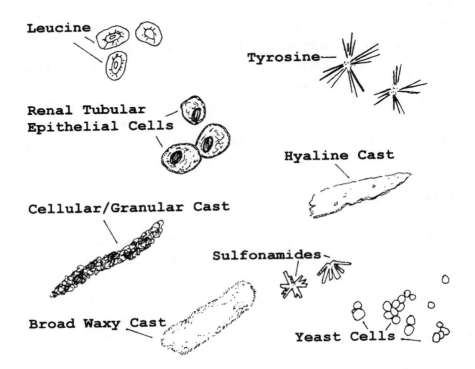

Leucine

Tyrosine

Renal Tubular Epithelial Cells

Hyaline Cast

Cellular/Granular Cast

Sulfonamides

Broad Waxy Cast

Yeast Cells

The Importance of Monitoring Kidney Function

It makes sense that tests for monitoring kidney function such as urinalysis is one of the first requested by a physician when a patient is seen. Much later in the disorder, when renal failure is present, an anemia and an imbalance of body electrolytes occurs. When these test results are seen, the patient is already seriously ill.

Additional information can be found in Sister Laurine Graff, *A Handbook of Routine Urinalysis* (Philadelphia: J. B. Lippincott, 1983); Susan King Strasinger, *Urinalysis and Body Fluids* (Philadelphia: F. A. Davis, 1985).

chapter 9

Histotechnology

Section 1. The Pathology Department

What Goes on in a Pathology Department?

The pathology department in a hospital is located near the clinical laboratories. The histotechnology laboratory, where tissues are prepared for microscopic examination, usually adjoins this department. Physicians who practice in this section of the clinical laboratory are called pathologists.

Pathology literally means the study of disease. When tissues are removed by means of a surgical procedure, they are processed in a histotechnology laboratory. Autopsy tissues from postmortem examinations are treated in the same way. That is, all tissues are examined and described visually and anatomically by a pathologist. Then, the pathologist cuts small representative sections for microscopic examination. Finally, glass slides containing sections of tissue microns thick from individual patients are examined microscopically. After carefully examining all sections of tissue from a patient, a pathologist makes a diagnosis.

The Histotechnologist

Histotechnologists are the clinical scientists who prepare tissues for microscopic viewing by a pathologist. The tissues have been processed by an automated system that passes them through chemical baths to preserve their structure. They are mounted in a paraffinlike substance and sliced seven microns thick. Then, they are automatically passed through solutions of dyes that prepare them for microscopic examination. When the tissues are seen with a microscope, pathologists can make a diagnosis based upon the examination of all slides connected with each surgical or autopsy case.

The Pathology Report

The pathology report describes any abnormalities of the tissue caused by a disease. The findings are described in detail and reported in the form of a diagnosis. The diagnosis and any accompanying remarks are sent to the attending physician. These surgical reports become a permanent and confidential part of a patient's medical record. When the tissues from an autopsy are examined, the cause of death is described and reported.

SECTION 2. HISTOCHEMICAL STAINING OF TISSUES

A staining procedure routinely performed on all tissue sections is the H and E. The H is for hematoxylin dye, which stains the nucleus, and the E is for eosin dye, which stains the cytoplasm of cells. In some instances, this routine stain shows some tissue changes of an early disorder but not conclusive proof. For the proof, a special histochemical stain may be used. Another section of tissue is prepared with a special staining procedure that demonstrates the suspected diagnosis.

An example of this is the acid-fast stain for the bacteria that cause tuberculosis. The organism is difficult to see with the H and E stain, so acid-fast staining is used to expose the pathogen in lung tissue or in the patient's expectorant. Numerous histochemical stains are performed by histotechnologists to demonstrate disease in muscle tissue, brain tissue, connective tissue, and even bone. This positive proof of the presence of these tissue changes makes it easier for a pathologist to determine the cause of disease.

chapter 10

Cytotechnology

SECTION 1. THE PAPANICOLAOU METHOD

An Overview of Cytotechnology

The cytotechnologist is a clinical laboratory scientist whose task is to examine smears of body fluids for inflammation, precancerous tissue changes, and cancer cells. There are several methods used to prepare the cellular harvest of different body tissues and organs by the Papanicolaou method (explained below).

Usually, a smear of body fluid is collected by a physician with a swab or automatic pipet and spread on several glass slides. A preservative that kills the cells is applied. After inserting them in a portable slide container, the slides are sent to a private clinical laboratory or hospital cytology laboratory to be examined by a cytotechnologist.

In the cytology laboratory, the cellular material on the

slides must be biochemically stained and examined. This procedure is named after the person who originated it in the 1940s, Dr. George N. Papanicolaou. It is commonly called a "Pap smear," using the first three letters of his name. Most women have a Pap smear yearly. As a result, precancerous lesions of the vagina, cervix, ovaries, and uterus can be detected early.

As mentioned, cells can be taken from any area of the body where disease is suspected. However, the most common location to remove cells for this test is the female reproductive tract. Some other sites where cells are obtained include heart, lung, thyroid, cerebrospinal fluid, urine, sputum, stomach contents, and cyst fluid. An additional way of obtaining specimens is by imprints made on glass slides of liver, spleen, or lymph node biopsies. In all of these preparations, cellular changes are looked for that suggest an inflammatory or malignant process. The cytotechnologist who examines these slides knows the normal configuration of these body tissues, cells, and fluids so that abnormalities can be identified and reported.

SECTION 2. THE TEST BEGINS

Making the Slides

Cells from the vaginal-cervical area as well as other parts of the body are cast off from organs or tissues with our natural secretions. This fluid is gathered and so are cells that have been gently scraped from the surface of organs or tissues. After an automated staining process, the glass slides are examined by a cytotechnologist.

Preanalytic Quality Control

After the smear is made, the slides are placed in a protective shipping case and sent to a cytotechnology laboratory. A cytotechnologist removes and examines them to determine whether they are suitable for processing. If a slide is broken, the physician is notified, and another one is requested so that reliable tests can be performed and reported.

Several conditions would cause them to be rejected by the cytotechnologist, including insufficient material for a representative sample, air drying has damaged the cells, or foreign substances obscure the important areas. This is part of the quality-control procedure that applies to cytotechnology.

The Thin Preparation of a Pap Test

A new method for collecting and preparing cervical samples, the thin-layer technique, eliminates making the smear. A small plastic brush is used to collect the cells and then placed in a small tube of liquid preservative. This protects the cells and lyses (dissolves) any red blood cells that may be in the sample. The sealed tube is sent to a cytology laboratory.

In the laboratory the cells are processed for viewing on a glass slide. The processing instrument draws up the liquid with the cells, leaving behind any debris. It deposits the cells on a slide in a small circle with very little overlap so that each cell can be examined. The slide is stained by the traditional Papanicolaou method and examined by a cytotechnologist.

SECTION 3. THE TEST

The magnification is one hundred for the first viewing. Then, for closer scrutiny of suspicious cells, a magnification of 450 is used. A search for cells that show inflammation, precancerous changes, cancer, or bacteria and parasites begins as the cytotechnologist looks at all elements present.

The entire slide is viewed for enlarged, dark, or irregular cell nuclei. Currently, computer-assisted Pap smear–screening devices eliminate a certain number of "normal" slides in which the cells have no signs of pathology.

In suspicious cases, the types of cell structure and pattern are graded according to a classification system used universally by cytotechnologists. When precancerous or cancerous cells are found, the smears are reexamined by a pathologist. To finalize a diagnosis, it may be necessary to obtain additional specimens from a patient. Sometimes a biopsy is required. When it has been verified that precancerous or cancerous cells are present, the patient is notified, and a course of treatment is begun.

SECTION 4. THE CYTOTECHNOLOGIST'S REPORT

Reports for cervical and vaginal cell pathology are classified according to the characteristics of normal or abnormal cells that are examined. Several methods of reporting these observations are used by cytotechnologists. One of them is the Bethesda System (TBS). When completed by a cytotechnologist, it provides an explanation of the findings on the smears.

Additional information can be found in Lynda Rushing and Nancy Joste, *Pap Smears* (Amherst, NY: Prometheus Books, 2002).

chapter 11

Molecular Biotechnology

SECTION 1. WAYS OF OBSERVING OUR HEREDITY

Cytogenetic testing, which maps a person's chromosomes from the cells in a drop of blood, has made great strides during the past two decades. Presently, however, it is possible to discover actual hereditary genes and find out their function. Genes are the units of inheritance located on a chromosome. Some latent diseases, those that we do not see early evidence of, can be recognized by studying our genes. These diseases include cystic fibrosis and some types of diabetes.

DNA Technology: How This Knowledge Affects Us

Two types of testing for finding out our heredity, DNA, have been mentioned and are used today. They provide us with valuable information about a person's chances of having certain disorders. As time goes on, these technologies will help us to avoid them.

The gene for hemophilia, a disease in which blood does not clot normally, has been recognized. Congenital diseases of newborns that result from abnormal chromosomes inside their cells can be detected. Thalassemia and sickle cell disease, both anemias caused by abnormal forms of hemoglobin, can be diagnosed by examining an individual's DNA. The possibility of a woman developing breast cancer is also discovered by gene study. Ongoing research promises the discovery of genes that cause other diseases. There will be a brief discussion of these technologies later in this chapter.

More about Cytogenetics

The branch of genetics concerned with the structure and function of the chromosomes in a cell is called cytogenetics. All of our chromosomes can be demonstrated by means of a map called a karyotype, a systematized array of the chromosomes in a cell. The cell has been captured in one of the stages of cell division (mitosis). We can use blood cells for this purpose. After culturing the blood cells they are examined with a microscope. One cell is found that is in a certain stage of cell division in which the chromosomes are widely dispersed. A computerized image is made of the chromosomes. This mixed display is arranged in pairs according to their size and shape, from the largest to the smallest. Any abnormality of the shape or number of the chromosomes is noted. There are known chromosomal patterns for some diseases, which makes these disorders identifiable. When a karyotype is produced by a cytogeneticist, an analysis of one's

A typical female karyotype

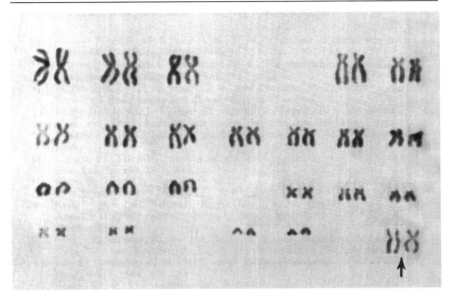

chromosomal makeup has taken place and any abnormalities are detected.

SECTION 2. WHAT IS DNA?

Now our focus is on a small part of the chromosome, the gene. The entire sum of one's deoxyribonucleic acid is called a genome, which is divided into smaller parcels of DNA called chromosomes. They are in the nucleus of all body cells. These little gene packages determine the characteristics we give to our offspring.

The chromosomes are composed of molecules that make up our DNA. DNA is in the form of a double helix containing phosphates, sugars, and biochemical bases. These units of heredity, or genes, are similar to tiny computers that store large amounts of information and instructions. It is important to remember that the order of the biochemical bases controls all the activities in a cell. If the order of molecules is changed, the DNA code will be changed.

A Brief Biochemistry Tour

The backbone of DNA consists of phosphates and sugars. Each deoxyribose sugar is connected to one of four bases that are in pairs. They are adenine (A), guanine (G), cytosine (C), and thymine (T). The bonds connecting the phosphates and sugars are not easily broken by chemicals. However, the bonds between base pairs of two opposite strands of DNA are easy to break by heat. The result is two separate strands. This process is called denaturation. The strands recombine upon cooling.

Where Does Ribonucleic Acid (RNA) Come In?

Each chromosome in the nucleus is a single strand of DNA containing thousands of genes. The genes have the code for making proteins, which are distinctive for each kind of cell in the body. This is the interesting part. The coded information in our DNA provides the formula for the protein. This information is carried from the nucleus to the cytoplasm of each cell by a messenger type of RNA. When information in the RNA is used to form a protein, the coded message has been read. The protein that the particular type of cell makes is produced in its cytoplasm.

Mutations of a Chromosome

When mitosis (cell division) takes place, a copy of the original DNA goes to each of the two resulting daughter cells. To do this, the DNA splits and new identical strands are formed. During this process, if one of the bases pairs with the wrong base, permanent hereditary changes occur called mutations.

Mutations can also occur when there is a deletion or a missing base. A mutation occurs when the DNA is broken by x-rays or by environmental factors, then rejoins in the wrong way. When these mutations happen in crucial genes, illness can result.

SECTION 3. HEREDITY

How Do We Inherit Our Individual Characteristics?

We have forty-six chromosomes in each of our body cells. Chromosomes are intricately packed to fit into the nucleus. Since they are composed of DNA, they are the heredity mechanism that ensures that our genetic code remains complete when our cells divide.

Mitosis goes on all the time in our bodies because tissue cells of all types are needed for all our body functions. If cell division did not take place, for example, we would be unable to grow, repair injuries, or digest food. Of course, when the cell divides, the result is a split of the cytoplasm and the cell nucleus. Each new nucleus contains an identical set of chromosomes. So every time a cell divides, each daughter cell receives a copy of the DNA from the original cell.

Analyze a Chromosome and Find Genes

A gene is a region of DNA that encodes one function. Genes carry specific information about the amino acid sequences—hereditary factors—unique for the protein of each person. The result of gene activity is seen in our physical characteristics. "Invisible" gene activity is our body biochemistry. Some disorders are detectable by testing for genetic markers, which are characteristics that can be traced to a particular gene.

Our Share of Genes

A combination of genes from a father and a mother results in the characteristics of each person, for example, the traits of brown hair and blue eyes, a tall stature, or the probability of diseases such as diabetes and cancer are in our genes.

Each Person Receives a Share

The offspring receive a set of genes from each parent, but the type of gene action is important. For example, in a set of two genes, one may be dominant over the other. In the experiments in which inheritance was discovered by Gregor Mendel, green pea seeds had the characteristics of round or wrinkled. The round seed shape was a dominant trait represented by R. The wrinkled seed was a recessive trait represented by r.

The dominant gene trait of the pair will be seen in the offspring. The recessive trait is seen only when both parents (or seeds when peas are grown) contribute a recessive gene for that trait. A simple diagram demonstrating this is seen here.

Simple Table of Heredity Patterns with Dominant/Recessive Traits

first generation RR vs. rr				second generation Rr vs. Rr		
	r	r			R	r
R	Rr	Rr		R	RR	Rr
R	Rr	Rr		r	Rr	*rr*

R=dominant   r=recessive

In *rr*, the recessive trait is observed. The recessive trait is observed in the second generation as a result of two recessive inherited genes.

SECTION 4. CHARACTERISTICS OF DNA USEFUL IN TESTING

We know that the DNA content of a cell is found in the chromosomes. As previously mentioned, the interactions that keep the DNA in this form are easily disrupted by biochemical means so the strands can be unwound and separated when analyzing it. This denaturation process is accomplished when high temperatures or when a high pH is applied to a cell culture.

Denaturation is reversible, so the formation of double-stranded DNA from different chains of single-stranded DNA is possible. The term for this is renaturation or hybridization. In this way, two single strands of DNA or one strand each of DNA and RNA can be combined if desired. In other words, hybrids are the reassociation of DNA strands that were not original partners. This process is not easy to accomplish because extended time periods are required and complex testing procedures are used.

SECTION 5. ANALYTIC APPROACHES TO DNA TESTING

There are several techniques for analyzing a DNA molecule. One is gel electrophoresis, which you are familiar with from the clinical chemistry chapter. The fragments of DNA migrate at different rates in the gel of the electrophoretic instrument and are measured. From this the nucleic acid sequence is determined.

The second process is hybridization analysis, which also has been described. A combination of hybridization and probes (DNA fragments labeled with radioisotopes or antibodies) are used to investigate biological fluids and tissues to diagnose disease. Probes combine with a complementary nucleic acid target inserted into the test system, thus identifying the disease or a microorganism. Applications of probe technology include prenatal and postnatal diagnosis of genetic diseases and the identification of a father in paternity cases.

An Amplification Technique— Polymerase Chain Reaction (PCR)

This procedure is familiar to us because of the publicity it has received in connection with criminal investigations. PCR produces large numbers of copies of DNA sequences selected for a certain reason. Some of them are used to screen for common genetic disorders or to examine blood stains in forensic tests. But these copies of DNA fragments are used mainly to find matching sequences for fast identification of unknown or mysterious sequences.

DNA probes and PCR make it possible to discover infections by microorganisms, including *E. coli*, *Shigella*, *Neissaria*

270

gonorrheae, Chlamydia trachomatis, M. tuberculosis, and *P. carinii.* Viral pathogens that can be detected by these methods are rabies, hepatitis B and C, HIV, polio, cytomegalovirus, human papilloma virus, herpes simplex virus, and adenovirus. This technology allows us to treat patients earlier and more effectively. The method used for identifying the culprit in these infections depends upon the time the various bacteriological, immunochemical, or serological procedures require to produce a definitive answer.

Restriction Fragment Length Polymorphism

Another method of studying DNA is the restriction fragment length polymorphism (RFLP) test. It allows scientists to map genes to find their locations on chromosomes. The genes for several disorders have been found with this technology— Huntington's disease on chromosome 4, cystic fibrosis on chromosome 7, and Alzheimer's disease on chromosome 21.

SECTION 6. GENETIC ENGINEERING—WHAT IS IT?

Genetic engineering makes use of the DNA characteristics described. It is a deliberate altering of genes within or between species for various reasons. The result is a modification and recombination of genetic material to create new gene combinations. The scientific term for this is recombinant DNA. You are familiar with the term *clone*, which is used to describe a colony of identical cells or organisms carrying a recombinant DNA fragment. Sometimes this technique helps us produce new gene products or substances that are hard to obtain in pure amounts.

An Example

We have found out by understanding our physiology and cell biochemistry the precise protein deficiencies responsible for such metabolic disorders as diabetes, hemophilia, and dwarfism. They can be corrected by supplying the missing or underproduced protein such as insulin for diabetes, clotting Factors VIII and IX for hemophilia, and human growth hormone for dwarfism. These substances are produced in limited amounts by the body, even though more might be needed by some individuals.

By using DNA technologies, we can produce therapeutic proteins from cloned human genes inside bacterial hosts. This eliminates the risk of virus contamination and allergic sensitivity that could occur when these therapeutic proteins are isolated from animals such as cattle or pigs. The protein harvested from the bacterial culture that is used for this purpose has been formed from a human coding region and is identical to the original protein. Human insulin that results from recombinant DNA technology is good for humans with diabetes. In this case of genetic engineering, the bacterial cells used are *E. coli.*

Uses for Molecular Tests

Forensic Tests for Identification

In forensic testing, PCR techniques can help identify individuals at the scene of a crime. The cells used for analysis may be from samples of hair, blood, or saliva or may be skin and reproductive cells.

When a criminal suspect is apprehended, specimens of tissue are obtained. The DNA fragments from the crime scene are compared with the DNA of the suspect when his tissue is prepared in the same way. If they match, there is a high probability that the suspect perpetrated the crime.

The HIV-PCR Test

Another example of putting this new technology to good use is the recently developed HIV-PCR test, which uses PCR to detect the human immunodeficiency virus. We can confirm the presence of the disease and detect viral infection much earlier. The body takes several months to produce detectable antibodies. The HIV-PCR test does not depend on antibody detection. It tests for the presence of the DNA of HIV.

SECTION 7. GENE THERAPY—HOW CLOSE ARE WE?

We can diagnose genetic diseases, but the means of treating them needs more research in the fields of gene enhancement or replacement therapy. The means of replacing genes or changing them in living persons is not practical at this time. The body or somatic cells of a person who has a genetic disorder can be treated with gene therapy, but this correction is not passed on to future generations.

So far, progress in gene therapy research has been made on diseases of the bone marrow and blood, including sickle cell anemia and thalassemia. The procedure for gene therapy in one of these disorders is withdrawal of a bone marrow sample from a patient. The replacement gene is accepted by the marrow cells, and the bone marrow cells are then cultured. The patient undergoes radiation to destroy the diseased marrow. Then, the "repaired" marrow cells are reinjected into the patient. These cells travel through the blood circulation to repopulate the bone marrow, resulting in normal red blood cells. If all goes well, the disease has been defeated.

Additional information can be found in Robert F. Weaver and Philip W. Hedrick, *Basic Genetics* (Dubuque, IA: William C. Brown, 1995); Edith Zak Helman, *Recombinant DNA Basics: A Primer* (Berkeley, CA: Berkeley Scientific Publications, 1993); David A. Micklos and Greg A. Freyer, *DNA Science* (Cold Spring Harbor, NY: Cold Springs Harbor Laboratory Press, 1990); Desmond S. T. Nicholl, *An Introduction To Genetic Engineering* (Cambridge: Cambridge University Press, 1994).

Glossary

analyte—the chemical or biochemical substance in a specimen of body fluid of any type that is measured by testing in a clinical laboratory.

antibody—a protein substance developed by cells of the body's immune or defense system against a foreign substance. They interact with microorganisms of different kinds, parts of cells, or other substances that stimulated their production. The antibody is formed in response to a protein antigen and interacts specifically with that antigen.

anticoagulants—substances that prevent the blood from clotting. They usually do not enter into or impede biochemical reactions that take place in a test. If in rare instances they will interfere, the clinical scientist requests that a suitable anticoagulant is used for collecting the specimen.

anticoagulated blood—blood that does not clot because of a chemical's presence. Different-colored rubber plugs indicate to a phlebotomist which chemical is present. If plasma is needed for testing, clot formation is prevented by using an anticoagulant. The tube of blood is centrifuged to propel the blood cells to the bottom. Plasma is the fluid in the tube above the cells. An anticoagulant is used when studying blood cells or when testing for biochemical substances in plasma.

antigen—a protein substance that stimulates the production of specific antibodies by the immune system.

autoimmune—describes a disorder in which the patient's own immune system attacks and damages tissues and organs.

automated cell counter—an instrument that directly measures the number of white blood cells, platelets, and red blood cells, in each microliter of blood. The mean corpuscular volume (MCV) and hemoglobin are also measured. A microcomputer in the instrument calculates the hematocrit, mean cell hemoglobin (MCH), and mean cell hemoglobin concentration (MCHC). The entire group of these tests is called the automated complete blood count (CBC).

azotemia—a condition in which waste products from our metabolism accumulate in the bloodstream. The kidneys have lost their capacity to filter waste products from the blood efficiently. This results in increased plasma creatinine, urea nitrogen, and uric acid test values. These substances should be eliminated when the kidneys function normally.

blood clotting (coagulation)—these are common terms for hemostasis, which literally means "stoppage of blood flow." This is important because it prevents blood from escaping when we are injured. The coagulation cascade in terms of body physiology is shown and described in the chapter on coagulation.

blood smear—a valuable diagnostic tool for clinical scientists and physicians. The presence of anemias and leukemias are usually evident when viewed on a well-prepared Wright's stained blood smear examined by a clinical scientist. A detailed explanation of a differential white blood cell count, performed on a blood smear, is provided in the test section of the hematology chapter.

diabetes mellitus—a disease having to do with our body physiology in which carbohydrates cannot be used. Diabetes is caused by a deficiency of insulin. If not treated, water and electrolyte loss occurs with serious illness.

diuretic—an agent that causes increased urine excretion. Common substances that do this are tea and coffee. Some prescribed drugs have the same effect, so electrolyte testing is performed periodically.

enzyme—a protein whose structure has biochemical sites capable of speeding up chemical reactions. Enzymes act in the body where important jobs must be done efficiently. Clinical testing for enzymes is vital because they are present inside all body cells and are essential for normal body function. Two examples of enzymes are lactate dehydrogenase (LD) and alkaline phosphatase (ALP).

fasting specimen—a sample of body fluid taken when no food is consumed for twelve to fourteen hours before phlebotomy is performed for clinical laboratory testing. Usually water may be taken.

glucose (sugar)—an energy-producing carbohydrate. When the body's biochemical actions for using glucose malfunction, the disorder is called diabetes. Glucose is consumed in many foods, such as candy, fruit, and baked goods. The starches we eat are converted to sugar by enzymes in saliva and in the stomach before they can be fully digested.

glucosuria—when glucose is present in urine because there is too much glucose in the bloodstream for the kidneys to retain. Therefore the excess glucose (sugar) is excreted in the urine. This indicates to a physician that the patient needs further testing.

hemodialysis—a procedure that involves the use of an artificial kidney. Blood from an artery of the patient is pumped through cellophane-like tubing with a balanced salt solution on one side and blood on the other. Because the patient's blood is outside the body, heparin is added to it so that clotting does not occur. The small and large molecules moving across the permeable membrane of the tubing allows for the removal of waste products. The purified blood is returned to the patient's circulatory system.

hemolytic anemias—a group of anemias in which the survival of red blood cells is shorter than the normal life span of 120 days. Examples of this type of anemia are thalassemia and sickle cell anemia.

hemolytic—a process in which red blood cells are destroyed in the circulation. This can happen when the red blood cells course through the circulatory system or as they pass through the spleen or liver. RBC destruction usually leads to an anemia referred to as hemolytic because the RBCs are being lysed (destroyed).

hyperglycemia—a higher-than-normal blood plasma level of glucose.

hypoglycemia—a lower-than-normal blood plasma level of glucose.

parenteral—the introduction of nutrients into the body by means of veins or subcutaneous tissues, avoiding the stomach and intestinal tract.

pathogen—a microorganism capable of causing an infectious disease. The microbe could be a bacterium, virus, parasite, or fungus.

plasma—the fluid part of the circulating blood that does not contain the cellular portion. It is obtained by centrifuging a sample of anticoagulated blood in a test tube. The cells of the blood remain in the bottom of the test tube. The fluid above the cells is plasma and is removed with an automatic pipet.

reagent strips—used in urinalysis testing and in point-of-care testing when speed is important. The strips are impregnated with chemicals that react with urine or plasma to detect one or more analytes present. Some of these are sugar, bilirubin, protein, and bacteria. A color change on the reagent strip provides an estimate of the amount of these substances in the specimen.

reference range—often called the normal range, gives the upper and lower limits of test values accepted as normal when measured in a representative healthy population for a locality.

screening tests—measure elements of body fluid that may be causing illness in the physician's estimation. They are requested of the clinical laboratory after a physical examination and a family history of disease has been obtained.

When certain screening test values are positive, more specific tests are requested to discover the cause of illness. An example of a screening test is the complete blood count (CBC).

serum—the fluid portion of blood that has been allowed to clot in a test tube. The clot, which takes the shape of the test tube, shrinks over a period of several hours, expressing straw-colored serum. The cells of the blood are trapped in the fibrin clot.

uremia—a toxic condition that results from retention in the blood of biochemical waste products normally excreted by the kidneys. Uremia is the result of severe kidney failure.

Appendixes

APPENDIX A—SYSTEMS AND ANALYTES

blood system, 35
blood group and Rh antigens, 224, 228
coagulation, 73
electrolytes, 142
enzymes, 114
gastrointestinal, 164
genitourinary, 166
immune, 199
insulin and sugar, 90
integument, 169
lipids, 124
liver and gallbladder, 107
protein, 131
renal, 98
respiratory, 158
thyroxine, 137

APPENDIXES

The clinical chemistry chapter includes some systems of the body that produce or metabolize certain minerals and biochemical compounds essential for our health. These compounds, or analytes, are briefly discussed at the beginning of the chapter (p. 87).

APPENDIX B—CLINICAL TESTS

HEMATOLOGY

antinuclear antibody test, 210, 211
body fluid examination, 50
bone marrow examination, 51
complete blood count (CBC), 52
differential white blood cell count, 52
electrophoresis, 53
hematocrit, 54
hemoglobin determination, 54
platelet (thrombocyte) count, 55
red blood cell count, 55
red blood cell indexes, 44
white blood cell count, 55

COAGULATION

activated partial thromboplastin time, 80
bleeding time, 80
coagulation factor assay (analysis), 81
prothrombin time, 81
thrombin time, 81

CLINICAL CHEMISTRY

acid phosphatase (ACP), 121–22
alanine aminotransferase (ALT), 117–18
albumin, 133
alkaline phosphatase (ALP), 119–20
aspartate aminotransferase (AST), 117–18
bilirubin, 109
calcium, 107
carbon dioxide, 145
chloride, 145
cholesterol, 128
clinical chemistry test panels, 89
C-reactive protein, 123
creatine kinase (CK), 122
creatinine, 98–99
globulin, 133–34
glucose tolerance test, 94–95
glycosylated hemoglobin, 96
HDL cholesterol, 127–28
lactate dehydrogenase (LD), 118–19
lipids, 130–31
liver disease, 110
pH of blood, 144, 145
phosphorus, 107
potassium, 143–44, 145
prostate specific antigen test (PSA), 121
protein electrophoresis, 134
sodium, 143, 145
thyroxine 3, 138, 142
thyroxine 4, 138, 142

troponin, 123
total protein, 132
triglycerides, 127
uric acid, 114
urea nitrogen, 98–99

MICROBIOLOGY

antimicrobial susceptibility test, 151–52
bacterial cultures, 154
differential biochemical reaction kit, 156
dry mount microscopic examination, 153
Gram stain, 153
parasite testing, 178
pinworm, 184
tapeworm, 183
trichinella, 185
viral cultures, 187–89

IMMUNOLOGY AND SEROLOGY

antinuclear antibody test, 210
enzyme immunoassay, 205–206, 220
fluorescent antibody test, 208, 221
immunodiffusion, 207–208
latex tests, 205, 221
precipitation reactions, 207
radioimmunoassay, 205, 221

Donor Collection Center and Blood Bank Laboratory

antibody screening test, 230–31
blood grouping (typing), 224–26
compatibility testing, 230
Rh testing, 228–30

Urinalysis

test procedures, 237–51

Histotechnology

tissue preparation, 254–55

Cytotechnology

cell examination, 260
cytotechnology procedure, 258–59

Molecular Biotechnology

cytogenetic procedure, 263–65
denaturation, 269
DNA analysis, 270
hybridization, 270
PCR, 270–71
recombinant DNA, 271–72

APPENDIX C—DISORDERS AND DISEASES

HEMATOLOGY

aplastic anemia, 56
autoimmune hemolytic disorder, 56
bacterial infections, 57
folic acid deficiency, 58
hemolytic anemia, 58
Hodgkin's lymphoma, 59
infectious mononucleosis, 60
leukemia, 61
lymphopenia, 62
malabsorption, 63
neutropenia, 64
pernicious anemia, 71
sickle cell anemia, 64–65
sickle cell trait, 66
systemic lupus erythematosis (SLE), 67–68
thalassemia, 68
viral infections, 69
vitamin B_{12} deficiency, 70

COAGULATION—BLOOD CLOTTING

disseminated intravascular coagulation (DIC), 82
Factor VIII deficiency (hemophilia), 83
Factor IX deficiency, 83
liver disease, 84
platelet deficiencies, 84
vitamin K deficiency, 84
von Willebrand's disease, 86

CLINICAL CHEMISTRY

acute kidney failure, 101–102
cholecystitis, 109, 111
chronic kidney failure, 101
coronary thrombosis indicators, 122–24, 129–30
diabetes mellitus, 91–92
gout, 113
hyperparathyroidism, 106
hyperthyroidism, 140
hypoglycemia, 93
hypothyroidism, 141
jaundice, 112
lipoprotein disorders, 129
malabsorption, 106
multiple myeloma, 136–37
proteins in kidney disease, 135
proteins in liver disease, 135–36
rickets, 105

MICROBIOLOGY AND IMMUNOLOGY/SEROLOGY

adenovirus, 189
amoebiasis, 179
anthrax, 159–60, 210
beta-hemolytic streptococcus, 160–61, 212
blastomycosis, 175
Candida, 174–75, 221
chlamydia, 168, 221
coccidioidomycosis, 175–76, 221
cytomegalovirus, 189, 220
diarrhea, 165–66, 217–18

flu, 161, 221
food poisoning, 164, 212
gastritis, 161–65, 214
giardiasis, 179, 221
gonorrhea, 168, 213, 221
hepatitis, 189–90, 214–15, 220
herpes, 190–91, 220, 221
histoplasmosis, 175
human immunodeficiency syndrome, 191–93, 215, 220
human papilloma virus, 193–94, 221
infectious mononucleosis, 193, 215–16, 220
influenza, 194, 221
Legionnaires' disease, 161, 221
Lyme disease, 170, 216, 220
malaria, 181–82
measles and mumps, 194, 220, 221
meningitis, 163, 216
pinworm, 184–85
pneumonia, 220, 221
rabies, 171, 195, 216–17, 220
ringworm, 174
smallpox, 195, 218
syphilis, 168–69, 218–19
tapeworm, 182–83
tetanus, 170–71, 219, 221
toxoplasmosis, 180–81, 220
trematode, 183–84
Trichinella, 185
Trichomonas, 179–80, 219, 220
tuberculosis, 162–63, 220
West Nile virus, 171, 196
whooping cough, 161

Index

acid phosphatase, 121–22

acne, 169

acquired immunodeficiency syndrome (AIDS), 191–93, 215, 220

activated partial thromboplastin time (APTT), 80

alanine aminotransferase (ALT), 117–18

albumin, 132–33
  functions of, 133

alkaline phosphatase (ALP), 119–21
  disorders of bone, 120
  disorders of liver, 121
  normal increases, 120

amoebic dysentery, 179

analytes measured, 26–27

anemias

classification of, 45–48
  macrocytic, normochromic disorders, 47
  microcytic, hypochromic disorders, 48
  normocytic, normochromic disorders, 46
  RBC indexes, 44–45
  RBC shape and volume, 43
  signs of, 42–43

anthrax, 159–60, 210

antibiotics, 151–52

antibodies, 200–201, 229
  formation of, 200–202

antigens, 200–201, 224–25, 228–29

antimicrobial susceptibility tests, 151–52

aplastic anemia, 56

INDEX

aspartate aminotransferase (AST), 117–18
autoimmune diseases, 211
autoimmune hemolytic anemia, 56–57
autoimmunity, 203–204

bacteria
antimicrobial susceptibility test, 151–52
bacterial resistance, 150
classification, 151
colonization, 148
good or bad, 148
host, 149
infection, 150
survival, 149
virulence, 149
bacterial infections, 57
beta-hemolytic strep, 160–61, 212
bile, 109
blockage, 109
forms of excretion, 109
jaundice, 112
products, 109
bilirubin products in urine, 241, 242, 247
blastomycosis, 175
bleeding time (BT), 80
blood ABO system, 224–26
blood type inheritance, 227
reverse typing, 226
tests for blood type, 226
universal donor, 225

blood bank laboratory/donor collection center, 223–24
antibody identification, 230–31
clinical laboratory tests in, 226, 228, 230, 232
compatibility test, 230
blood cells, 36–42
abnormal cells, 40
immature cells, 39–40
in urine, 246, 248
blood component separation (apheresis), 233
autologous transfusion, 231
component therapy, 234–35
plasma, 234
platelets, 234
red blood cells, 234
white blood cells, 235
blood disorders, 55–71
aplastic anemia, 56
autoimmune hemolytic anemia, 56–57
bacterial infections, 57
Celiac disease, 63
gliadin test in, 63
Crohn's disease, 63
folic acid deficiency, 58
hemolytic anemia, 58–59
Hodgkin's lymphoma, 59–60
Reed-Sternberg cell in, 60
infectious mononucleosis, 60–61
heterophile antibody test, 61
leukemia, 61–62

lymphopenia, 62
malabsorption, 63–64
neutropenia, 64
pernicious anemia, 71
sickle cell anemia, 64–66
sickle cell trait, 66
systemic lupus erythematosus (SLE), 67–68
thalassemia (Mediterranean anemia), 68–69
ulcerative colitis, 63
viral infections, 69–70
vitamin B_{12} deficiency, 70
blood, examination of, 37, 52–53
blood group antibodies, 224–25
blood group antigens, 224–25
blood proteins, 131
blood system, 35–37
bone marrow, 36
circulating blood, 35–36
blood tests, microscopic
complete blood count (CBC), 52
differential white blood cell count, 52–53
blood urea nitrogen (BUN), 98
body fluid examination, 50–51
bone marrow biopsy, 51–52
bone marrow examination, 51–52
botulism, 164, 212

calcium and phosphorus, 103–107
calcium and parathyroid, 106
control of, 104–105
disorders of
carcinoma of bone, 106
hyperparathyroidism, 106
rickets, 105
function, 104
metabolism, 104
reference range, 107
specimen collection, 107
test for, 107
Candida (yeast), 174–75, 221
casts and crystals
in urine, 249–50
cardiovascular event, 122–24
cardiac troponin, 123
C-reactive protein, 123
creatine kinase values in, 122
exclusion of, 124
risk factors for, 123, 128
Celiac disease, 63
gliadin test in, 63
chlamydia, 168, 221
chromosomes, 264–66
karyotype, 264–65
mutations, 267
clinical chemistry
introduction, 87
systems tested, 88
test panels, 89
Clinical Laboratory Improvement Act, 29
clinical laboratory licensure and accreditation, 29

clinical laboratory scientists, 20–21
  laboratory disciplines, 22–23
  types of certification, 28–29
clinical tests
  development of, 26
  why needed, 19
coagulation cascade, 75
coagulation disorders, 82–86
  disseminated intravascular coagulation (DIC), 82–83
  Factor VIII deficiency (hemophilia), 83
  Factor IX deficiency, 83–84
  liver disorders, 84
  platelet deficiencies, 84
  vitamin K deficiency, 85
  von Willebrand's disease, 86
coagulation factor assay, 81
coagulation factors, 73–74
  common pathway, 75–76
  deficiencies of, 77
  extrinsic pathway, 75–76
  final stages, 76
  intrinsic pathway, 75–76
  treating disorders, 77
coagulation, 73–86
  mechanism of, 73–74
coagulation, testing procedure, 77–79
coagulation tests, 80–82
  activated partial thromboplastin time (APTT), 80
  bleeding time (BT), 80
  coagulation factor assay, 81
  prothrombin time (PT), 81

screening tests, 78
  thrombin time (TT), 81
Coccidioides immitis, 175–76, 221
complete blood count (CBC), 52
C-reactive protein, 123, 205
creatine kinase (CK), 122
creatinine, 98–99
Crohn's disease, 63
cytomegalovirus (CMV), 189, 220
cytotechnology, 257–60
  locations for cell study, 258
  microscopic examination, 260
  Papanicolaou test, 257–58
  quality control, 259
  specimen collection, 258
  test report, 260
  thin preparation method, 259

diabetes, 91–93
  forms of, 91
  insulin-dependent diabetes mellitus (IDDM), 91
  non-insulin-dependent diabetes mellitus (NIDDM), 91
  physical effects, 92
  symptoms of, 92–93
  tests for, 94–96
differential white blood cell count, 52–53
disseminated intravascular coagulation, 82
DNA (deoxyribonucleic acid), 265–66
  biochemical characteristics, 269

composition of, 266
denaturation, 269
renaturation (hybridization), 269–70
DNA testing
  gel electrophoresis, 270
  hybridization, 269–70
  polymerase chain reaction (PCR), 270–71
  restriction fragment length polymorphism (RFLP), 271
donor collection center, 224
  blood preservation, 233
  donor screening, 232

ear infections, 169–70
E. coli, 165–66
electrolytes, 142–45
  bicarbonate ions, 144
  definition of, 142
  function of, 143
  hydrogen ions, 144
  pH, 144
  potassium, 143
  sodium, 143
  testing of, 145
endocrine system, 137
enzymes, 114–24
  acid phosphatase (ACP), 121
    PSA test, 121–22
  alanine aminotransferase (ALT), 117–18
  alkaline phosphatase (ALP), 119–21

aspartate aminotransferase (AST), 117–18
balance of, 115
daily tracking, 116–17
forms of, 115
increases of, 116
levels in blood, 115–16
measurement of, 114
stages of, 115–16

Factor VIII deficiency (hemophilia), 83
Factor IX deficiency, 83–84
fluke, 183–84
folic acid deficiency, 58
forensic testing, 272–73
fungi
  culture of, 173
  infection
    by blastomycosis, 175
    by Candida (yeast), 174
    by Coccidioides immitis, 175
    by Histoplasmosis, 175
    by ringworm, 174
  microscopic examination, 173–74
  mold form, 173
  yeast form, 172

gastritis or ulcer, 164–65, 214
gastrointestinal tract, 164–66
  infections of
    botulism, 164
    E. coli, 165

gastritis or ulcer, 164
   Salmonella, 165
normal flora, 164
gene study, 264, 268–69
genetic engineering, 271–72
gene therapy, 273–74
genetic markers, 268
genetic testing, 263
genitourinary tract, 166–69
infections of
   chlamydia, 168, 221
   Giardia lamblia, 179, 221
   gonorrhea, 168, 213, 221
   syphilis, 168–69, 218–19
normal flora, 466
globulin, 133–34
fractions of, 134
functions of, 134
glucose (sugar), 90
acceptable levels in serum, 94
in hemoglobin
   glycosylated hemoglobin (A_{1c}), 96–97
   reference range for glyco-hemoglobin, 96–97
hypoglycemia, 93
insulin, 90
oral glucose tolerance test, 95
specimen collection, 94–95
in urine, 97, 245
glycosylated hemoglobin (A_{1c}), 96–97
goiter, 141
gonorrhea, 168, 213, 221
gout, 113

Hashimoto's disease, 141
Helicobacter pylori, 164–65, 214
hematocrit, 54
hematology
disorders. *See* blood disorders
tests, 50–55
   body fluid examination, 50
   bone marrow examination, 51–52
   complete blood count (CBC), 52
   differential white blood cell count, 52–53
   examining blood smear, 53
   hematocrit, 54
   hemoglobin determination, 54–55
   hemoglobin electrophoresis, 53
   heterophile antibody test, 61, 215–16, 220
   making blood smear, 52
   platelet count, 55, 276
   red blood cell count, 55, 276
   screening tests, 49
   white blood cell count, 55, 276
hematuria, 246
hemoglobin, 41, 52, 53, 54
hemoglobin electrophoresis, 53
hemoglobinuria, 246–47
hemolysis, 56–57
hemolytic anemia, 58–59
hepatitis A, B, and C, 189–90, 214–15, 220

heredity, 267–69
  traits, 268
herpes, 190–91, 220, 221
heterophile antibody test, 61, 215–16, 220
histoplasmosis, 175
histotechnology, 253–55
  histochemical staining, 254–55
  histotechnologist, 254
  histotechnology procedures, 253–54
  pathology department, 253
  pathology report, 254
HIV (human immunodeficiency virus) tests, 191–93, 215, 220
Hodgkin's lymphoma, 59
  Reed-Sternberg cell, 60
HPV (human papilloma virus), 193–94, 221
hyperthyroidism, 140
hypoglycemia, 93
hypothyroidism, 141

immune response, tests for
  anthrax, 210
  autoimmune diseases, 211
  beta-hemolytic streptococcus, 212, 221
  botulism, 212
  C-reactive protein, 213
  gonorrhea (STD), 213
  Helicobacter pylori, 164–65, 214
  hepatitis A, 214, 220–21
  hepatitis B, 214–15, 220

hepatitis C, 215
human immunodeficiency virus (HIV), 215, 220
infectious mononucleosis, 215–16, 220
Lyme disease, 216, 220
meningitis, 216
rabies, 216–17, 220
rheumatoid arthritis, 217
Salmonella, 217–18
Shigella and E. coli, 218
smallpox, 218
syphilis, 218–19, 220
tetanus, 219, 221
Trichomonas vaginalis, 219, 220
West Nile virus, 219–20
immune system, 199–202
  antigens, 200–201
  antibodies, 200–203
  autoimmunity, 203–204
  Rh antigen, 201, 229–30
immunity
  active, 202
  passive, 202–203
immunoglobulins, 203–204
  source of, 203
  testing for, 204–205
immunology/serology, test methods
  agarose gel precipitation test, 207–208
  agglutination, 204–205
  antigen/antibody combinations, 205–207
  antinuclear antibody test, 210

chemical luminescence, 207
dye labeled, 205
enzyme reaction, 205–206
flocculation, 207
fluorescent antibody test, 208–209
latex, 205
precipitation, 207
radioactive isotope label, 205
immunology tests quick reference, 220–21
infection, 149–50
infectious mononucleosis (IM), 193, 215–16, 220
influenza, 194–95, 221
insulin, 90
insurers of health care, 31–32
CPT code, 31
local medical review policies (LMRP), 32–33
reimbursement, 31

jaundice, 112

kidney, 97–98
acute failure, 101–102
chronic failure, 101
function, 100, 276, 280
hemodialysis, 102, 278
importance of, 97–98, 238
protein disorders of, 135
signs of failure, 100
tests for function, 102, 103

lactate dehydrogenase (LDH), 118–19
Legionnaires' disease, 161, 221
leukemia, 61–62
leukocyte function, 38–39
abnormal forms, 40
in infection, 38–39
"shift to the left," 39
WBC count, 55, 276
leukocytes (white blood cells)
count, 55
granulocytes, 38–40
in immunity, 35
B lymphocytes, 40–41
immunoglobulins, 40–41, 203–204
T lymphocytes, 40
lymphocytes, 40–41
monocytes, 38
reference range, 55
lipids (fats), 124–31
common names and acronyms, 127–28
digestion of, 125
forms of, 126
specimen collection, 131
testing for, 130, 131
transport of, 124–25
lipoproteins, 126–27
benefits of some, 128
disorders of, 129
good and bad fats, 128
liver, 107–12
bilirubin, 109, 110, 111, 247

liver disorders, 111
    substances produced, 108
    tests for function, 110–11
Lyme disease, 170, 216, 220
lymphopenia, 62

malabsorption, 63–64
    screening tests for, 63
malaria, 181–82
    falciparum infection in, 181
    testing for, 182
measles, mumps, 194, 220, 221
meningitis, 163, 216
metric system, 21–22
microbiology
    dry mount test, 153
    Gram stain, 153
    methods of diagnosis, 147
    normal flora, 157
    presumptive report, 154
    specimen collection, 152
    testing procedures, 153
microbiology testing
    culture, 154
    identification system, 156
    observing growth, 155
microbiology test kit, 27
microscopic examination
    of blood, 52–53
    of urine, 248–50
mitosis (cell division), 264
morbidity, 150–51
mortality rate, 150–51
multiple myeloma, 136–37

neutropenia, 64

oral glucose tolerance test, 94–95

Papanicolaou test (Pap smear), 307
parasites, 176–85
    characteristics, 176–77
    definition, 176
    entry into host, 177–78
    flatworms, 182–84
        fluke, 183–84
        tapeworm, 182–83
        testing for, 183
    life cycles, 176
    protozoa, 179–82
        amoebic dysentery, 179
        falciparum infection, 181
        Giardia lamblia, 179
        malaria, 181–82
        testing for, 182
        toxoplasmosis, 180–81
        Trichomonas, 179–80, 219
        testing for, 180
    roundworms, 184–85
        pinworm, 184
        testing for, 184
        Trichinella (trichinosis), 185
        testing for, 185
    survival in host, 178
    testing, 178
pernicious anemia, 71
    causes of, 71

tests for, 71
pinworm, 184
  test for, 184
platelets
  count, 55, 276
  deficiencies, 84–85, 86
  function, 41–42, 73–74
  reference range, 55
proteins, 131–37
  albumin, 133
  disorders of, 135–37
    AIDS, 135
    kidney disease, 135–36
    liver disease, 135–36
    multiple myeloma, 136–37
  globulin, 133–34
  immunoglobulins, 133–34
  importance of, 131
  origin of, 132
  reference ranges, 134–35
  testing, 134
prothrombin time (PT), 81
prostate specific antigen test (PSA), 121–22

quality control, quality assurance, 28–29

rabies, 171, 195, 216–17, 220
red blood cells (RBCs)
  hemoglobin, 41, 52, 53, 54
  morphology, 41
  RBC count, 276
  reference range, 55

renal system, 98
respiratory tract
  normal flora, 158
  infections of, 159–63
    anthrax, 159–60
    influenza, 161
    Legionnaires' disease, 161–62
    meningitis, 163
    streptococcus, 160–61
    tuberculosis, 162–63
    whooping cough, 161
  pathogens, 158
Rh, 228–30
  antibody formation, 229
  antigens, 228–29
  immune globulin, 230
  in pregnancy, 201, 229–30
rheumatoid arthritis, 213, 217
ringworm, 174
RNA (ribonucleic acid), 266

Salmonella, 165, 217–18
sexually transmitted diseases (STDs), 167–69
  chlamydia, 168, 221
  damage caused by, 167
  gonorrhea, 168, 213, 221
  syphilis, 168–69, 218–19
screening tests, 49, 78
Shigella and E. coli, 165–66
sickle cell anemia, 64–65
  blood circulation in, 65
  differential WBC count in, 65

hemoglobin S, 65
sickling, 65–66
test for hemoglobin S, 66
test for sickling, 66
sickle cell trait, 66
skin (or integument)
  infections of
    acne, 169
    ear infections, 169–70
    skin boil, 169
  normal flora, 169
skin barrier infections, 170–71
  Lyme disease, 170
  rabies, 171
  tetanus, 170
  West Nile virus, 171
smallpox, 195, 218
Streptococcus, 160–61, 212
syphilis, 168–69, 218–19
systemic lupus erythematosus (SLE), 67–68
  autoimmune hemolytic anemia of, 56, 67
  clinical findings, 67
  lupus erythematosus cell (LE cell), 68
  tests for, 68

tapeworm, 182–83
  testing for, 183
test classifications, 29–31
  Class I, 30–31
  Class II, 30–31
  Class III, 29–30

testing, at home, 26–27
test samples, origin of, 25–26
tests as devices, 25
  microbiology test kit, 27
tests, screening, 52, 78
tetanus, 170–71, 219, 221
tetraiodothyronine (T_4), 138
thalassemia (Mediterranean anemia), 68–69
  tests for, 69
thrombin time (TT), 81
thyroid gland, 137–42
  control of secretions, 139–40
  disorders of, 140–41
    goiter, 141
    Hashimoto's disease, 141
    hyperthyroidism, 140
    hypothyroidism, 141
    pituitary malfunction, 141
  endocrine system, 137
  function, 137
  iodine absorption, 138–39
  tetraiodothyronine (T_4), 138
  thyroxine, 138
  triiodothyronine (T_3), 138
  testing, 142
thyroxine, 138
toxoplasmosis, 180–81, 220
  testing for, 180
Trichinella (trichinosis), 185
Trichomonas, 179–80, 219, 220
triiodothyronine (T_3), 138
tuberculosis, 162–63, 220

uric acid, purines, 112–14
  gout, 113
  metabolism, 112–13
ulcerative colitis, 63
universal donor, 225
urea
  BUN, 98
  creatinine, 98
  production, 98
urinalysis
  importance of, 237–38
  parts of, 241–42
urinalysis (the test), 241–50
  bilirubin (bile), 247
  blood
    hematuria, 246
    hemoglobinuria, 246–47
  blood cells, 248
  casts and crystals, 249–50
  glucose, 245
  ketones, 246
  microscopic examination, 248–50
  nitrite, 247
  pH, 241, 242, 243
  physical characteristics, 241
  protein, 244–45
    high values in, 245
  quality control, 240
  reagent strips, 241–42
  specific gravity, 243–44
  specimen collection, 239–40
  twenty-four-hour specimen, 238–39

venipuncture, 35
viral infection, blood tests for, 69–70
viruses, 186–96
  alternative entry paths, 187
  characteristics of, 186
  culture of, 188–89
  identification of, 189
  infections of, 69, 189–97
    common cold, 189
    cytomegalovirus (CMV), 189
    hepatitis A, 190
    hepatitis B, 190
    hepatitis C, 190
    herpes, 190–91
    HIV (human immunodeficiency virus), 191–93
      course of disease, 192
      path of entry, 192
      testing for, 193, 215, 220
    HPV (human papilloma virus), 193–94, 221
    infectious mononucleosis, 193, 215–16, 220
    influenza, 194, 221
    measles, mumps, 194, 220, 221
    rabies, 171, 195, 216–17, 220
    smallpox, 195, 218
    West Nile virus, 171, 196
  path of entry, 186
  specimen collection, 187

vitamin B$_{12}$ deficiency, 70
  anemia of, 70
vitamin K deficiency, 85
von Willebrand's disease, 86

white blood cells (WBC). *See*
  leukocytes
whooping cough, 161